John Kenrick

A Selection of Papers on the Subjects of Archæology and History

communicated to the Yorkshire philosophical society

John Kenrick

A Selection of Papers on the Subjects of Archæology and History
communicated to the Yorkshire philosophical society

ISBN/EAN: 9783337242565

Printed in Europe, USA, Canada, Australia, Japan

Cover: Foto ©Andreas Hilbeck / pixelio.de

More available books at **www.hansebooks.com**

PAPERS

ON SUBJECTS OF

ARCHÆOLOGY AND HISTORY,

BY THE

REV. JOHN KENRICK, M.A., F.S.A.

A SELECTION OF PAPERS

ON SUBJECTS OF

ARCHÆOLOGY AND HISTORY,

COMMUNICATED TO

THE YORKSHIRE PHILOSOPHICAL SOCIETY,

BY

The REV. JOHN KENRICK, M.A., F.S.A.,

CURATOR OF ANTIQUITIES.

LONDON:
LONGMAN, GREEN, LONGMAN, ROBERTS, & GREEN.
YORK:
R. SUNTER, STONEGATE; J. SOTHERAN, CONEYSTREET.
1864.

The Papers collected in this Volume were communicated to the Yorkshire Philosophical Society, and are now published with their sanction. Some of them were read at their Monthly Meetings; others were Lectures delivered to more numerous assemblages of the Members. This will explain the variety of subjects to which they refer. They will be found, however, to have one character in common. Their object is rather to excite an interest in Archæology, by pointing out its relation to History and Literature, than to pursue antiquarian, historical, or literary research into minute detail. The wish expressed in the last Annual Report of the Society, that they should be preserved in a permanent form, leads me to hope that this object has been in some measure attained.

J. K.

TABLE OF CONTENTS.

		Page
1.	The Rise, Extension, and Suppression of the Order of Knights Templar in Yorkshire . . .	1—68
2.	The Historical Traditions of Pontefract Castle, including an Inquiry into the Place and Manner of Richard II.'s Death	69—99
3.	The Relation of Coins to History, illustrated from Roman Coins discovered at Methal near Warter, and presented to the Yorkshire Philosophical Society by the late Lord Londesborough and W. Rudston Read, Esq.	100—127
4.	The Causes of the Destruction of Classical Literature	128—156
5.	The History of the Recovery of Classical Literature	156—181
6.	The Reign of Trajan illustrated by a Monument of his reign found in York	182—197
7.	Roman Waxed Tablets found in Transylvania .	198—216
8.	New Year's Day in Ancient Rome .	217—237

I.

THE RISE, EXTENSION, AND SUPPRESSION OF THE ORDER OF KNIGHTS TEMPLAR[1] IN YORKSHIRE.

ALTHOUGH the special purpose of this paper is to illustrate the history of this celebrated order in reference to our own county, some notice of its origin and organization is necessary in order to explain its peculiar constitution, and the relation in which it stood to that state of European society out of which it arose.

The characteristic of the order of Templars, as of the kindred order of the Knights of the Hospital, was the combination of religious enthusiasm with military ardour, of monastic discipline with military service. Its institution was the immediate fruit of the Crusade, which had made the Christians masters of the Holy City, and its origin is to be sought in the same feelings, and the same constitution of society, as gave birth to the Crusades themselves. These lay deeper than the ardent zeal of Peter the Hermit, or the outrages of the Turks on pilgrims to the Holy Sepulchre, or the policy of the Popes, desirous to acquire new lands for the domain of the Western Church. The elements of that religious and military excitement, which jointly impelled the people of Europe to throw themselves in such

---

[1] The title of the order varies in English writers,—"Knight Templars," "Knights Templars," "Knights Templar." I shall in future call them simply Templars.

myriads on Asia, were found in the character and habits which the northern conquerors had brought with them, and which civilization had only partially tempered. In the governments which they had founded out of the ruins of the Roman Empire, everything had been military. The possession of landed property, political rights, even the security of personal freedom, depended on the power to use arms. This military spirit had hitherto found occupation at home, in aggression or defence; but in the eleventh century the increasing power of the sovereign, and the general progress of social institutions, had greatly lessened the sphere of domestic warfare, while the successive invasions of the barbarous tribes, which for many centuries kept Europe under arms, had entirely ceased.[1] The Crusades were therefore the natural fruit of the military spirit and system of life which had prevailed in Europe, and the limitation of its field of action at home.

The direction of this spirit to a religious object was also in accordance with the temper of the times. We find Christianity assuming different characters in the countries in which it was embraced, according to the genius and circumstances of the people. The mystical and contemplative Egyptian retired to the Desert of the Thebaid, and introduced, or transplanted from the shores of the Dead Sea, the solitary and monastic life. The intellectual Greek employed the resources of his subtle language and metaphysics, in speculations on the persons

---

[1] The introduction of Tournaments, which belongs to the same century as the Crusades, (see Sismondi Hist. des Français, 3, 110,) is an indication of the restriction of the sphere of private warfare, and the cessation of barbarian inroads.

and operations of the Godhead, and in framing hypotheses for combining Christian doctrine with heathen philosophy. The warriors of the West, when they heard of their Saviour's sufferings, laid their hands upon their swords, and wished they had been present to rescue him. They never troubled their practical minds with the refinements of theology, or entertained any question about the evidences of their faith, but they were ready to hazard their lives in battle against a heretic or an infidel. The ardent zeal and military enthusiasm of the western nations were concentrated and inflamed by corresponding feelings and similar institutions on the part of the Mohammedans, who possessed the Holy Land, and were in constant warfare with the Christians in Spain. They, too, were warriors, believing with all the fervour of ignorance in the divine mission of their prophet, and the sacred duty of propagating his religion by arms. The Christian and the Mohammedan differed in their notions of Paradise, but they agreed in thinking that the surest road to it was by death in battle with an unbeliever. The hell of one, and the Jehannum of the other, was the certain destiny of him whom they respectively called an infidel or a Giaour.

The Crusades thus naturally gave rise to the military orders, which united monastic vows and a mode of life partially monastic, with the profession of arms. The state of the newly acquired conquest of the Holy City called for some vigorous exertion. The great leaders had taken possession of their several kingdoms of Antioch, Damascus, and Edessa;

the inferior knights had settled themselves comfortably in their castles, and the sovereign of Jerusalem had not sufficient military strength alone to protect the pilgrims from the West, or the unarmed population of his kingdom. The Bedouins ventured from their deserts; the Seljuk Turks and Egyptians still ravaged the country, and the idle rabble which had accompanied the Crusaders, or been attracted by their conquest, preyed upon the peaceful inhabitants.[1] It was impossible to perform the offices of hospitality to the pilgrims, unless they were protected by the strong arm, and the brethren of the earlier institution, the order of St. John Eleemon, Patriarch of Alexandria, (afterwards changed to St. John the Baptist,) whose special office it was to attend upon them, were also knights. They owed their origin to merchants of Amalfi, who resorted to Palestine to vend their goods, and at the same time visited the Holy Sepulchre.[2] The conception of a new order, more exclusively military than that of the Hospitallers, originated with two French knights, Hugo de Payens (de Paganis) and Godefroi de St. Omer (Galfridus de Sancto Audemaro), with whom seven other French knights associated themselves.[3] The vow taken by these nine founders of the order was to give themselves to the service of Christ, to live without personal property (sine proprio), and according to the rule of the Canons Regular, in chastity and obedience, and to guard the public

---

[1] Wilke Geschichte des Tempelherrenordens, vol. 1, p. 12.
[2] Dugdale, 6, 2,798.
[3] Matthew Paris sub an. 1118. According to some they were "ex infimis Hospitaliorum congregati," which cannot have been true of the founders of the order. Hist. Angl. Script., col. 1008; Gul. Tyri Archiepisc., 12, 7.

roads. This last was in truth its special duty at its institution. The utility of the order was immediately perceived by King Baldwin II., the patriarch, and the Christian nobility, and Hugo de Payens was dispatched to France, to engage the Pope, the King of France, and, above all, St. Bernard, in their cause. At this time St. Bernard's voice was even more potential in Europe than that of the Pope. From his monastery at Clairvaux he exercised an influence, which a few years later (A.D. 1146) enabled him to rouse the West to a new Crusade; and the celebrity which he had gained as a reformer of monastic discipline naturally directed the founders of the new order to him, as the fittest man to establish its Rule, and to recommend it to the patronage of the great. To him Baldwin sent a letter by two brothers of the order, Andrew and Gundemar, to bespeak his favour and his influence, and to ask him to frame them such statutes as should combine the religious with the military life. At the same time the two founders of the order, accompanied by several of the brethren, proceeded to Rome to engage the patronage of the Pope, Honorius II. A Council was held at Troyes in Champagne in 1128, at which the order was formally established, and the rules sanctioned which St. Bernard had drawn up.

In the interval between the time when the foundation of the order was laid at Jerusalem and its recognition by the church, its members had occupied, by the permission of Baldwin II., a part of his palace, supposed to be built on the site of Solomon's Temple. They depended in great measure on his bounty for food, clothing, and armour, and their style and title was "pauperes fratres militiæ J. C.,"[1] or "Templi Salomonis," whence the name of Templars. Till they had a church of their own they used the church of the Holy Sepulchre,[2] which had been built by the Empress Helena, and was sometimes called Templum Domini. The patriarch of Jerusalem, under whose immediate superintendence the Templars were placed, was designated Patriarch of the Church of the Holy Sepulchre. Such was Heraclius, who in 1185 dedicated the Temple Church in London, according to an inscription still to be read there. At their foundation the Templars deserved the title of "Poor Soldiers of Christ." Their whole property appears to have been their arms and horse-furniture, and they had no distinguishing costume. But from the time of the Council of Troyes the order rapidly increased in numbers and wealth. The seed had been dropped into a soil containing the elements of luxuriant growth.

The Statutes which St. Bernard gave them are

---

[1] Matthew Paris says, "Adeo pauperes erant (Hugo et Godefridus) ut unum tantum equum haberent communem, unde eorum sigillo insculpuntur duo equites, uni equo insidentes!" Dugdale's editors, 6, 2, 787, say this of the Hospitallers. Is there any authentic seal of either with such a device?

[2] It is commonly said that the round form, still seen in the Temple Church, London, at Northampton, Cambridge, and Maplestead, is owing to the connexion of the Templars with the church of the Holy Sepulchre at Jerusalem, which had this form. But with the exception of London, the Templars do not appear to have been connected with any of the places in which round churches remain. Gough, indeed, in his additions to Camden (2, 19), says that Temple Bruére in Leicestershire, and Aislaby in Lincolnshire, had round churches, but neither of them appears to have been standing in his time. See an Essay by Rev. Geo. Poole in Reports of the Church Architectural Societies of York, Lincoln, &c., 1850 — 1, p. 235.

said to have been founded on the Benedictine rule, but they bear manifest traces of the Cistertian reform, of which he was a zealous patron, so that Bernardine is sometimes used as a synonyme for Cistertian.[1] As we have them, however, they indicate a somewhat later origin than the time of St. Bernard, but no doubt in all important points they are such as he dictated them to his amanuensis, John of Alamaton. They are curious as exhibiting the methods which it was thought might be effectual, in combining things so incongruous as the monastic and the military life. Every knight was to attend upon the holy offices at the regular hours, but if prevented, he was to say thirteen *pater-nosters* for missing matins, nine for missing vespers, and seven for each of the other hours. A special exemption from matins was made in behalf of those who had been fatigued by military duty, but they were required in this case to chant thirteen prayers. They were not to exhaust their strength by too long standing at prayers; after the *Venite exultemus* they might all sit down; but were required to stand up again at the *Gloria Patri*, at the recitation of the Gospels, the Te Deum, and the Lauds. Holy reading was always to take place at meals in the refectory: flesh was permitted only three times a week, except at Christmas, Easter, and the Feast of the Virgin. Two dishes were allowed on Sunday to the knights and chaplains, but the squires and servants were to be content with one. To preserve equality, the knights were to eat in pairs. After Complin a collation was allowed, it being left to

---

[1] The Statutes are given at length by Wilke, vol. 2, p. 203.

the discretion of the master to determine, whether water only should be drunk, or a competent portion of tempered wine. The garments of the knights were to be white (it was not till the papacy of Eugenius III., the disciple of St. Bernard, that they assumed the red cross);[1] those of the inferior members black, or a dark colour. Furs were forbidden, but lambs' or sheep's skins might be worn in winter. Their clothes were to be of a simple make, so that they might dress and undress themselves readily. All superfluous ornaments of dress, and boots and shoes curved at the toes,[2] were forbidden, as heathenish and abominable, to the knights, and not allowed even to the servants. Hawking and shooting with the bow or cross-bow were prohibited; no knight was even to go in company with one who carried a hawk. Some other regulations seem more suited to a rather strict boarding school than an association of warriors. They were not to go into the city without leave, except by night to the Holy Sepulchre, or the stations without the walls. They were to go to bed, " vestiti camisiis et femoralibus," not to sleep two in a bed, except in case of extreme necessity; a light was to be constantly burning in the dormitory; a pillow, a piece of sacking, and one

---

[1] Gul. Tyr., 12, 7.
[2] Sect. 24. "De rostris et laqueis." See Du Cange, sub voc. From *laqueus* comes our lace. The rostrum is thus described in a Latin mediæval poem, quoted by Du Cange:—
"——— Deductior ante
Pinnula procedit, pauloque reflexior exit,
Et fugit in longum tractumque inclinat acutum."
They were forbidden to monks and clergy by several councils and synods. The fashion seems to have been introduced from Constantinople.

coverlet, were to suffice for each; their shirts were to be of linen from Easter to All Saints; woollen during the winter months. No letters were to be written to or received from parents or relatives, nor any present to be accepted from them, but by permission of the Master or Procurator. With these formal regulations many useful precepts for maintaining peace, order, and good will, were mingled, and the knight was specially warned against what might endanger the observance of his most difficult vow. "Fugiat fœminea oscula Christi militia, per quæ solent homines sæpe periclitari." The prohibition extended to a mother or a sister. Altogether St. Bernard shows himself a master of monastic discipline, and had persuaded himself that it might be combined with a military life; but this lay beyond his experience, and it is not wonderful that his ideal Templar, if he ever existed, very soon degenerated. He endeavoured to persuade the secular knights to exchange into this order, by an epistle, in which he set forth the immense advantage of dying in a religious cause rather than a secular quarrel. The secular knights, he says, are clothed in flowing garments, their dress and armour decorated with gold and gems; they wear long hair, after the manner of women, and make war either to gratify their passions or from the love of aggrandizement. The Templars, on the contrary, live frugally, make no distinction of persons, never use insolent language or idle jesting, shun field sports, cut their hair short, never comb[1] and seldom

[1] This was a Roman military virtue. "Caput *intactum buxo* maresque pilosas, Adnotet, et grandes miretur Lælius alas." Juvenal, Sat. 14, 194.

wash themselves, trust to steel, and not to gold on their armour for victory, and seek to mount strong and fleet horses, only that they may be effective for battle. (S. Bernardi Opera, vol. 1. p. 545.)

The new institution accorded with the religious and military spirit of the times, and it spread rapidly through the West. Its founders travelled through France, England, and Spain, and found everywhere liberal support. Hugo had an interview with Henry I. in Normandy, whence he passed into England and Scotland, gathering such a number of men to go to Jerusalem, as had not gone "since the days of Pope Urban," in the first Crusade. More than three hundred knights accompanied Hugo de Payens on his return, with an unnumbered crowd of squires and servitors. They found ample occupation for their arms, for the infidels had been gaining ground upon the Christians. There was seldom a battle in which the Templars were not engaged, and in the siege of Damascus they were almost entirely cut off. The eloquence of St. Bernard produced a second Crusade, conducted by Conrad III. and Louis VII. in 1145. It was unfortunate in its issue. The Christian army was defeated before Damascus, and treachery was imputed to the Templars.[1] Historians in general, however, lay the blame upon the barons of Palestine, who were jealous of the Crusaders, though they had come to their assistance. That no such imputation justly rested on the Templars, in the opinion of Christendom, is evident from the great increase of their wealth which took place about this time. Roger de

[1] Hist. Angl. Script., A. D. 1147.

Mowbray, whose name we shall find as the donor of some of their richest endowments in Yorkshire, must have known their character, as he had taken part in the second Crusade.[1] In the long contest with the Infidels, the Templars appear to have been the chief strength of the Christian forces. It was their privilege to carry the true cross before the army when it went to battle, as well as the banner with the red cross inscribed on it.[2] They occupied the post of danger—the van in advance, the rear in retreat. As they were the flower of the chivalry of Europe, and accomplished in all military exercises, they acted as officers to the troops whom they were enabled to hire by means of the wealth which Christendom poured into their coffers. The footing which they obtained in all the kingdoms of Europe, within a century after their establishment, is characteristic of the age. Many a man who felt no vocation to leave his home and fight in Palestine, and yet acknowledged the duty of endeavouring to keep possession of the Holy Sepulchre, would compromise with his conscience, by giving land or money to the soldiers of Christ. Many a devout lady, who regretted that she could not, like Erminia or Clorinda, mingle in the fray of arms, would joyfully endow the gallant knights who were fight-

---

[1] Dugdale, Baronage, 1, p. 122. A singular privilege was granted to him and his heirs, that of releasing a Templar from public penance. Addison, p. 47.

[2] Their original banner was black and white, and was called *Beauseant*, which became their war-cry. It was used of piebald horses. Du Cange, Baucens. The meaning of the mixture of colours is uncertain. May it not have alluded to the original co-operation of the Hospitallers, whose dress was black, with the Templars, who wore white? *Bausen* is used in Scotch for a piebald horse. See Jamieson's Dict. sub. voce.

ing for the recovery of the Holy Land. Many a conscience, touched by gratitude for a mercy received, or remorse for a sin committed, would feel relief in the idea, that the debt to heaven might be paid, or its displeasure averted, by a donation or a bequest to the Templars. The foundation of religious houses went on *pari passu* with the endowment of the military orders. Rievaulx, Fountains, Bolton, Kirkstall abbeys, as well as several priories, were founded in Yorkshire in the course of the 12th century.

The earliest grants which we find made to the Templars in England are of the reign of Stephen, A. D. 1135—1154. He gave them certain manors for the salvation of his own soul, and that of his wife Matilda, and his son Eustace, and his uncle Henry. Matilda herself was also a benefactress to the Templars.[1] The house of the order in London was at this time just without Holborn Bars, near Southampton Buildings. Henry II. gave them a site on the Flete (then not a ditch, but a river flowing rurally from Hampstead,) for the construction of a mill, and also the Church of St. Clement Danes. The increase of their wealth led them to erect a splendid house and church on ground which they purchased, extending along the Thames from the Monastery of the Whitefriars as far as Essex Street. Heraclius, the Patriarch of Jerusalem, consecrated it in 1185. He visited Europe in consequence of the Christians having suffered a great defeat from Saladin, but returned without accomplishing much by his journey.

It was probably the visit of Heraclius which led

---

[1] Dugdale, Monasticon, 6, 2, p. 838.

to a general survey of the lands and rents of the order; for it was in 1185 that Jeffrey, by whom this survey was made, undertook the office of Preceptor of the Ballia de Anglia, or Master of the Temple. In the organization which the order had now attained, England was divided into a number of balliæ, and in every place where they had considerable possessions, they established superintendents, called in this country *preceptors* (receivers), in foreign countries more commonly *commendatores*, whence commanders and commanderies. The preceptors in the provinces were subject to the Grand Preceptor or Master of the Temple in London, who both held chapters there at which the provincial preceptors appeared, and also made visitations throughout England. He was in his turn subject to the Grand Master whose residence was at Jerusalem, but who occasionally held chapters at Paris, where the representatives of the order from the kingdoms of the West assembled. The balliæ mentioned in this survey are London; Kent; Warwick (which was of great extent, going as far as Launceston); Weston, near Stevenage in Hertfordshire; Lincolnshire;[1] Lindsey; Widine (South Witham, near Colsterworth, on the borders of Leicestershire); and finally, Eborascire, Yorkshire.

The great benefactors of the order in this county were the families of De Lacy, De Brus, De Mowbray, De Roos, De Stuteville, De Courtenay, and Hastings. Of the position which they held in the

---

[1] The three-fold division of this county is indicative of the large possessions of the Templars in it. Dugdale's Baronage, 1, p. 123, 125.

aristocracy of the North we may form an idea from the circumstance, that Robert de Brus, Roger de Mowbray, Robert de Stuteville, and Ilbert de Lacy, were all present in the great battle of the Standard, near North Allerton, fought in Aug. 1138, in which the northern barons defeated David, King of Scots. Robert de Brus possessed Skelton and fifty other lordships in the north Riding, and forty-three in the East and West. It was his son, Adam de Brus, who was so liberal to the Templars; the father had founded Guisborough Priory, and been a liberal donor to the Abbey of Whitby, to Middlesburgh, and to St. Mary's at York. The famous Roger de Mowbray, Earl of Northumberland, lost his estates for rebelling against Stephen; but Nigel Albini, who married his daughter, took his name and his lands. Besides endowing the Templars richly from his Lincolnshire property, he gave them lands at Thorp near Catterick, at Thirsk, and at North Cave. He had been taken prisoner by Saladin in 1187, at the same time with Guy de Lusignan, the King of Jerusalem, at the fatal battle of Tiberias, which was followed by the sack of Jerusalem, and having been ransomed by the Templars, he showed his gratitude to the order by the ample donations which he made to them.[1] The family of De Roos took their name from Roos in Holderness. Robert, the second lord, the benefactor of the Templars, lived in the reigns of Richard I. and John. He was brother-in-law, and through his wife co-heir, of Walter Espec, the founder of Rievaulx Abbey. He gave them Ribston, Hunsingore, Cattal, and

[1] Dugdale Monasticon, 6, 2, p. 839.

Walsford. Alan Carpentarius endowed Ribston with lands at Cowthorpe, where the venerable oak may even then have stood. The De Stutevilles were a very ancient family in Yorkshire, having possessions in the East and West Ridings. The forest of Knaresborough belonged to them, and one of them makes a great figure in the history of St. Robert of Knaresborough, whom he first persecuted, and afterwards patronized, in the reign of King John.

The possessions of the De Lacys extended not only through many parts of England, but into Wales and Ireland. Gilbert, who in the reign of Stephen gave large donations to the Templars, after serving in the Holy Land became himself a knight of the order. His brother, Henry de Lacy, was one of the most powerful nobles of his day, possessing seventy-nine knight's fees and a half. The Honour and Castle of Pontefract belonged to the De Lacys, and they had wide lands in its vicinity. Henry gave to the Templars the Church of Kellington near Pontefract, and confirmed the donation of Whitkirk and Skelton near Leeds, with Newhusum or Nehus as it is called (Temple Newsome), originally given by William de Vilers.[1] William and Roger de Hastings gave to the Templars the lands of Hurst near Snaith, in the parish of Birkin, which retain the names of Temple Hurst, with the ruins of a preceptory. John de Courtenay

---

[1] The deed of donation is addressed to Roger, Archbishop of York, and the motive is stated to be "pro salute animæ meæ et pro animabus patris mei et matris meæ et omnium amicorum meorum, tam vivorum quam mortuorum, ut perhennis vita nobis omnibus donetur."

made a donation of lands at East Hurst, which still bear the name of Hurst Courtenay.

The following list of their possessions in Yorkshire has been made out partly from the survey of the different balliæ in 1185, partly from an enumeration by Stillingfleet in 1434, more than a century after the suppression of the order and the transference of their possessions to the Hospitallers.[1] From unpublished sources, no doubt, it might be enlarged.

Stratford	Stratforth, or Startforth, opposite to Barnard Castle.
Broctune	Brotton.
Gildale	Kildale.
Hengelbe	Ingleby.
Houkeswell	Hawkswell near Leyburn.
Karletun	Carlton near Arncliff.
Richemund	Richmond.
Wiltun	Wilton.
Careltune	Carlton near Stanwick.
Burgum	Brough near Catterick.
Pennel	Penhill.[2]
Cuton	Temple Cowton.
Stainhow	Stanghow near Guisborough.
Langtoun	Great Langton.
Jarum	Yarm.
Bartune	Barton St. Mary's near Croft.
Leibrunne	Leyburn.
Kirdintune	Kirklington near Sinderby (?)
Thimelby	Thimbleby.
Baggabi	Bagby.
Jernewic	Gervick near Skelton, N. Riding (?)
Lundhuse	Lund in the parish of Hawes.
Torp	Thorp near Burniston.

[1] Dugdale, 6, 2, 830, 838.
[2] The remains of an oratory belonging to the Templars were excavated here a few years since, and a farm is called Temple-Farm.

Watlous	Thornton Watlas.
Soureby	Sowerby near Thirsk.
Trese	Thirsk.
Burnebam	Burniston (?)
Aldefeld	Oldfield near Studley.
Lindebi	Lindrick near Ripon (?)
Scurventune	Scruton.
Leeming Bridge	Where Leeming Beck joins Swale.
Brunton	Patrick Brompton.
Honetune	Hunton near Patrick Brompton.
Fleta	Kirby Fleetham.
Apeltune	Appleton-on-Wisk.
Burel	Burrell near Bedale.
Crachall	Craik-Hall, Bedale.
Alawarthorpe	Allerthorpe, Bedale.
Osegotebi	Osgodby, near Thirsk.
Cukewald	Coxwold.
Kerebi	Cold Kirby.
Ampelford	Amplcforth.
Stainegrive	Stonegrave.
Calvertune	Cawton near Gilling (?)
Wimbeltune	Wimbelton near Harum.
Nuningtune	Nunnington.
Healmesley	Helmsley.
Scalletune	Scawton.
Haitun	Hayton, East Riding.
Cattun	Catton.
Pontem Belli	Stamford Bridge.
North Cave	North Cave.
Droitune	Drewton.
Withele	Whitley.
Baggaflete	
Ripplinham	Riplingham near South Cave.
Walebi	Waldby.
Clif	Cliff.
Wihetoft	Willetoft near Bubwith.
Faxflete	Faxfleet.
Kelintune	Kellington.
Fenwic	Fenwick near Campsall.
Hyrst	Temple-Hurst.

Ribstane	⎫
Cowthorpe	⎪
Hunsingore	⎬ Still retaining the same names.
Cattal	⎪
Wetherbi	⎪
Ilkei	⎭
Neuhusum	⎱ Temple Newsome.
Newbiggin	⎰
Whitchirch	Whitkirk.
Skelton[1]	
Wynhill	Winmoor.

Tanner[2] says the Templars had a priory at North Ferriby, founded by Lord de Vesci, which was afterwards converted into a priory of Austin Canons, at the dissolution of the Templars. Mount St. John near Thirsk has sometimes been reckoned among their possessions, but it seems from the first to have belonged to the Hospitallers. Their possessions at York were not splendid. They consisted of the Castle-mills, which existed till very lately, given by Roger Mowbray; Henry de Fishergate held them at a rent of twenty marks; three tofts, which the knights had purchased, for which Silvester paid four shillings; a toft on the other side of Ouse, for which Walter the Smith paid two shillings; and divers tenements in Conynge Street, given by Robert de Ros. They had also lands and a house

---

[1] In Dugdale, Monasticon, 6, 2, p. 841, is a grant from Hauwisia de Granteville of a bovate and toft in Skelton and another in Wynhill, "Ad sustentationem luminariæ beatæ Mariæ in capella ejusdem loci." Skelton adjoins Newsome.

[2] Notitia Monastica, p. 680. I do not find North Ferriby mentioned in either of the surveys of the property of the Templars in Yorkshire. In Dugdale, p. 803, note (°), a charter of King John is cited, by which he grants to the Templars land at Newland. The text, however, says, "to the Hospitallers," who certainly had a preceptory there. Newland is on the Calder, not far from Normanton.

and chapel at Copmanthorpe, where a field still bears the name of Temple-Garth. Westerdale near Guisborough, Etton near Beverley, and Alverthorpe near Wakefield, are mentioned among the lands transferred from the Templars to the Hospitallers,[1] though not included in the above list.

In looking through the list of the Templars' possessions in Yorkshire, we cannot fail to be struck with the variety and minuteness of the sources of their revenues. Besides carrucates and bovates of land, we find the right of holding markets, advowsons of churches, and medieties of rectories, multure from wind and water-mills, tributes of poultry, eggs, and swine, services of so many days in the year for ploughing, harrowing, haymaking, sheep-washing and shearing, mending ditches, and leading stones. They enjoyed rights of free warren, fisheries, and turbaries, and the manorial or baronial prerogatives of sac and soc, and tol and theam, and infangethef and utfangethef, &c. They also enjoyed many valuable immunities. A charter of Henry III.[2] grants them exemption from aids, danegeld, and horngeld, with a variety of imposts the precise nature of which it is difficult to ascertain, from stallage and pontage, from all forced labour on royal parks, castles, or palaces, and allows them to take timber freely from their woods, without impeachment of waste, and to essart (clear) those which they possessed within the limits of the royal forests, without leave of the royal bailiffs. The same charter gives them all waifs and strays on

---

[1] Larking, Knights Hospitallers in England, p. 141. [2] Dugdale, p. 844.

their lands not followed and claimed, and the goods and chattels which any of their men might have forfeited by crime, and allows them, in case of any of their tenants forfeiting his fee, to take immediate seisin of it, although the king had a right to keep it in his hands for a year and a day. Amerciaments incurred by any of their men, and carried to the exchequer, were to be given up to the Templars. They exercised jurisdiction not only over their own body, but over their tenants, and levied forfeitures.[1] A document preserved among the records of the Vicars Choral of York Minster[2] shows how desirous they were of extending their jurisdiction, to the exclusion of the ordinary tribunals. It is a bond by which Peter Middleton of Nesfield near Ilkley, who had disputes with the tenants of the Templars in Wharfedale, undertakes, under a penalty of twenty shillings, to be paid towards the fabric of St. Peter's at York, that neither he nor any of his tenants should take proceedings against the Templars in any court, canonical or civil; that he would not avail himself of any right of appeal that might be prejudicial to them; and that if he was injured by any of their tenants, he would bring his cause before their court at Whitkirk. This was an usurpation which might well excite the jealousy of the courts of law.

The order had been favoured by the Church as

---

[1] Dugdale. "Homines de Kercbi dicunt quod de omnibus placitis suis quæ non possunt finiri per illos, nisi per fratres, debent habere dimidium forisfactum et fratres dimidium aliud."

[2] I owe the communication of this document to the kindness of the Rev. Mr. Metcalfe, one of the Minor Canons of York Minster. It were to be wished that these records were given to the public. The bond in question is printed in full in the Gentleman's Magazine, Dec. 1857, p. 645.

well as by the Crown. Alexander III., in 1162, by his bull, called from its first words *Omne datum optimum* (Ep. James i. 17), had enacted that the Grand Master should be chosen by the collective order only, and that he should be already a Templar; that no Templar should be required to take an oath or do homage or fealty to any ecclesiastical or secular person; that the order should be free from the payment of tithes, but should be at liberty to accept tithes from clergy or laity with the consent of the bishop. The bishop was to be consulted, but if he refused assent, they might still be taken and retained by the Templars, on the authority of the Holy See. The most important privilege of all was that of receiving clerks and priests into the order, in their principal seat and in their dependencies, provided they were not members of any other order. Thus the cure of souls, and consequently an important means of control, was taken from the secular clergy. Another very important privilege which this bull conferred was, that if the Templars came to any city, castle, or village, in the course of their questing (ad suscipiendas collectas), which was lying under interdict, and in which consequently no divine service could be performed, the Templars' priest, if there were no church of their own, might celebrate mass in one of the churches of the place. This privilege the Templars are said to have grossly abused, and the synod held in the Lateran in 1179 made some stringent regulations designed to restrain both them and the Hospitallers, who had shewn a similar disposition to encroach.[1] Innocent III., who

---

[1] Wilke, 1, p. 82. Gervase in Script. x. p. 1451.

made a freer use of the weapon of the interdict and excommunication than any of his predecessors, found himself embarrassed by the privileges which they had granted, and addressed an epistle to the Grand Master[1] with the view of correcting the abuses of which the bishops had complained to him. In the same epistle he alleges, that they admitted into their fraternity any who would pay them a few pence annually, and for whom Christian burial might thus be claimed, though they died under interdict, or were persons of immoral lives—adulterers or usurers. In conclusion, he warns the Grand Master, that if a more strict discipline were not maintained and calamity should come upon the order, the fault would be their own.[2] Alexander IV. was more favourable to the Templars, and issued various bulls confirming all their privileges.

The reign of Henry III., which occupied fifty-six years of the thirteenth century, appears to have been the culmination of the power and wealth of the Templars. We may not be able to rely implicitly on the statement, that they possessed nine thousand manors and sixteen thousand lordships;[3] but the enumeration of their possessions in Yorkshire alone shows how large a portion of landed property they had acquired, and in France they were much richer than in England. Even here the Master of the Temple held his head high among the magnates of the land, and took his place in parliament, like the mitred abbots and priors.

---

[1] Wilke, 2, p. 240.
[2] Clement IV. had warned them, that without the protection of the Pope they would soon fall by the hostility of the bishops and the temporal princes. Addison, p. 391.
[3] Mat. Paris, p. 615.

Amaric de St. Maur was one of the high personages by whose advice King John granted Magna Charta. Yet this same century was full of disasters for them as defenders of the Holy Land. Jerusalem had been retaken in 1244; the Grand Master and the noblest of the knights had perished in the battle of Gaza; the Crusades had terminated in 1254 with the unsuccessful expedition of St. Louis. At the siege of Saphet in 1266, one hundred and thirty knights and seven hundred and sixty fighting men had been beheaded by the Soldan of Egypt, refusing to renounce their faith. By the capture of Acre in 1291, the last stronghold of the Christians in the Holy Land had been taken from them.

To the end the Templars maintained the character of valiant soldiers of the Cross, and there appears no ground for the imputation which Matthew Paris casts upon them,[1] that they might have conquered Palestine if they had chosen, but that they prolonged the war, in order to have a pretext for raising money in Christendom. But their position was invidious; their privileges encroached on the rights of the church and the prerogatives of the sovereign and feudal chiefs. Henry III., though he had favoured the order, had complained of their wealth and pride. "You prelates and religious," he says to the Grand Prior of England, "but especially you Templars and Hospitallers, have so many liberties and charters, that your superabundant possessions fill you with pride and madness. Those things, therefore, which have been hastily and imprudently granted by our predecessors, must

[1] Matt. Paris, p. 545.

be prudently and deliberately recalled. I will infringe both this charter and others, which I or my predecessors have rashly granted." The answer of the Grand Prior is haughty and defiant. "It be far from thee, O King, to utter such an absurd and ungracious word. As long as thou observest justice thou art a King; when thou infringest justice thou wilt cease to be so."[1] The rebuke was just, but both the strength and the pride of the order must have been great, when its chief ventured to hold such language to the sovereign. Though he does not appear to have fulfilled his threat of revoking his and his predecessors' charters, Henry bore a secret grudge against both Templars and Hospitallers, and endeavoured to do them mischief.[2]

It is not wonderful that distinguished and enriched as the Templars had been, their hearts should have been lifted up with the pride which goes before a fall. This is imputed to them as a characteristic vice. The anecdote is in all our histories, how Richard I. was advised by a bold preacher to quit himself of his three daughters— his Pride, his Avarice, and his Voluptuousness. "Your advice is good," said the King, "and I give the first to the Templars, the second to the Benedictines, and the third to my Prelates."[3] The Templars were not the worst matched of the three. Matthew Paris speaks of the "Templariorum superba religio."[4] Spenser, in his Prothalamion, speaking of the Temple buildings in London, says,

---

[1] Matt. Paris, p. 854.
[2] Matt. Paris, 862. "Ex aliis natis occasionibus Templariis et Hospitalariis insidias tetendit novercales."
[3] Hume, ch. 10.
[4] Matt. Paris, 517.

> "Where now the studious lawyers have their bowers,
> There whilome wont the Templar Knights to bide,
> Till they decayed through pride."

The profession of arms is one that does not foster a spirit of civil equality; the feudal system encouraged a contemptuous disregard of the humbler classes. But the Templars were the "cream of the cream" of European chivalry, and the *esprit de corps* of the order inflamed the pride which chivalry universally inspired. Their pride, however, does not appear to have shown itself in magnificent buildings; their preceptories, as far as we can judge from the few remains of them, at Temple Swingfield, at Temple Hurst, and elsewhere, were unostentatious. Indeed, as they were only transient occupants of their houses, they were not likely to expend much on their architecture or their ornament.

> "——— Their chiefest care
> Was horse to ride and weapon wear."[1]

No doubt wealth produced luxury as well as pride, but it was not confined to the Templars. Could St. Bernard have seen Prior Aymer of Jorvaulx and Sir Brian de Bois Guilbert, proceeding to the hall of Cedric, he would as little have recognized a Cistertian monk in the Prior, as a poor soldier of the cross in the knight. We read of an archdeacon of Richmond, who travelled with ninety-seven horses, twenty-one dogs, and three hawks,

---

[1] Pope Clement VI. complains of the Hospitallers, that the Hospitals in foreign parts derived little benefit from their great wealth; that they "equos magnos et pulchros equitant, cibis vacant delectabilibus, pomposis vestibus, vasis aureis et argenteis, et pretiosis aliis ornamentis utuntur; aves et canes tenent et nutriunt venaticos," and spent very little in almsgiving. Larking, p. lxix.

and of whom the Prior of Bridlington complains, that coming to a church of which they were the impropriators, he had cost them as much in one hour, as would have kept the whole convent a long time.[1]

Of the history of the Templars of Yorkshire, between the time of their establishment and their dissolution, scarcely any records remain. Their profession called them elsewhere, and we have no means of distinguishing them from the general body of soldiers of the cross in Palestine. The inhabitants of the Northern counties have always been remarkable for the qualities which belong to the military character. Their vicinity to the hostile kingdom of Scotland kept these qualities in exercise, producing at the same time a certain rudeness of manners and speech. The Templars could not be founders of families in which ancestral traditions of their exploits might have been preserved, but we may presume that the knights at least belonged to the aristocracy and gentry of the kingdom. Nor have we any detailed account of the manner in which their vast property was administered. Fortunately a record has been lately brought to light, which gives us a clear insight into the manner in which the Hospitallers managed their affairs,[2] and the circumstances of the two orders were so nearly alike, that probably the system of each was the same. Only a small number of the knights resided

---

[1] Gill Vallis Eboracensis, p. 70.

[2] "The Knights Hospitallers in England, being the Report of Prior Philip de Thame to the Grand Master, Elyan de Villanova, for 1338." Edited by the Rev. Lambert B. Larking, M.A., with an historical Introduction by John Mitchell Kemble, M.A. Printed for the Camden Society, 1857.

on the property belonging to the order. Some of the farms were let out to tenants paying rent; the larger properties were retained in their own hands, and cultivated by their servants and by the cottagers, who were bound to render a specified amount of service in husbandry. A variety of profits from smaller sources, as mills, tolls, fees of the courts which they assumed to hold, tithes of churches of which they were impropriators, fees from those in which they possessed an interest, the produce of quests,[1] swelled the amount of the income of the order. From this there were various sums to be deducted, for the maintenance of the establishment, for robes, arms, horse-furniture for the knights, expences of journeys, &c. What remained after the various reprises was paid to the general treasury. The larger properties were managed by the Preceptors, or the brethren next in rank to them; the smaller ones by bailiffs, but the Preceptors made periodical visitations. Among the expences of the Hospitallers we find considerable sums paid to lawyers, and even to the judges. The Templars were better able to protect themselves than the Hospitallers, but they too must have had suits to maintain in the King's Courts, and might find it for their interest to stand well with the Bench.

The commencement of the fourteenth century was marked by an event which precipitated the fall of the Templars. Acre had been taken in 1291. In conjunction with the Hospitallers they fitted out in 1300 an expedition from Cyprus, where they had established themselves after their expulsion

[1] See p. 21.

from Palestine, and took possession of the island of Tortosa.¹ But they were unable to hold it against the Soldan, and after losing many men, and leaving some in the hands of the enemy, they returned to Cyprus; and thus it became manifest, that all chance of recovering Palestine by means of the two military orders was at an end. They might have effected something, at least in checking the conquests of the Turks in the Egean and on the mainland of Greece, had they been united. The Popes were induced, both by enlightened views of policy and by the interest of the church, to cling to the hope of recovering the Holy Land, when sovereigns had renounced Crusades; and with this view they desired to preserve and strengthen the military orders. Gregory X. in 1274 had formed the plan of uniting the Benedictines and Cistertians in one order, the Templars and Hospitallers in another, and abolishing the Mendicants,² but died before it could be accomplished. Nicholas IV. again attempted this union in 1284 without success. A provincial council was held at York in 1291 to consider this plan, which was again frustrated by the death of the Pope.³ Indeed such had been the jealousy of the orders, and their acts of violence towards each other,⁴ that friendly co-operation for any length of time was hardly possible. It was proposed to the last Grand Master, Jacques de Molay, that the Templars should join the Hospital-

---

¹ Wilke, 1, 208, 224.
² Wilke, 1, 230.
³ Fasti Eboracenses, by the Rev. J. Raine, p. 339, note *j*.
⁴ Matthew Paris, p. 987. It should be observed that this writer is very unfriendly to the military orders, especially the Templars.

lers, who had taken possession of Rhodes, which they long rendered the bulwark of Christendom against the Turks; but the proposal was declined. Its acceptance might have saved the Templars, as it did the Hospitallers. Their office became a sinecure, and a plausible pretext was not wanting for the resumption of possessions and privileges, granted them for a purpose which they had ceased to fulfil. The sovereigns of Europe were beginning to free the crown from the checks which had hitherto impeded the growth of prerogative, and the Templars, who formed an almost independent power, an *imperium in imperio,* would be more obnoxious than ever, when their sphere of action was removed from the East, to the various countries of the West in which they had established themselves.

A powerful soldiery never terminated its existence by a peaceful dissolution. The Prætorian guards, who had so long tyrannized over the Roman emperors and people, were almost exterminated in the great battle which Constantine fought under the walls of Rome with Maxentius, to whom they adhered. It was easy, therefore, for Constantine to disband them, and distribute them among the frontier stations.[1] But it was only by massacre that Peter the Great could disembarrass himself of the Strelitzes, or Sultan Mahmoud of the Janizaries, or Mahmoud Ali of the Mamlooks. The late war with the Sepoys in India illustrates

---

[1] Jam obliti deliciarum Circi Maximi, et Pompeiani theatri, et nobilium lavacrorum, Rheno Danubioque prætendunt. Incert. Paneg. Constantini, cap. 21.

the truth, that it is only by some great catastrophe that a numerous and powerful military organization can be dissolved. The Templars had not even the consolation of dying with arms in their hands; they were the victims of treachery and chicane.

Notwithstanding some occasional antagonism, the Popes had hitherto steadily befriended the Templars. But this support was now to be withdrawn, and the Pope to become the instrument of their destruction. Pope Boniface VIII. and Philip-le-Bel (IV.) of France had been in bitter hostility; the death of the Pope was probably produced by chagrin at his arrest at Anagni, by order of Philip. His successor, Benedict XI., died by poison. The conclave of cardinals continued nine months after Benedict's death without being able to unite in the choice of a successor, so violent was the opposition of interests. The long suspense was terminated by the election of the Archbishop of Bourdeaux, who became Clement V. The support of Philip had been gained by a promise on the part of the Archbishop to fulfil six conditions, five of which were specified, and the sixth remained to be made known at the pleasure of the King.[1] Whether, even at this time, Philip had meditated the destruction of the Templars, and in his own mind made it the reserved condition, we do not know, but it is certain that in his proceedings against them he found a ready instrument in Clement. The plan itself was the conception of the King. He was one of the most unscrupulous of sovereigns—in an age when sovereigns generally made their own will

[1] Sismondi Hist. des Français, 6, 100, quoting Villani, lib. 8, c. 80.

the rule of right—cruel, faithless, and avaricious. His conduct towards Boniface had been violent and unjust. He had shown how little regard he had to individual rights, by confiscating the property of the Lombard bankers and threatening them with torture under pretence of their practising usury. Twice he had seized on the property of all the Jews, the second time banishing them from his dominions. Whether the Templars were guilty or not, we can have no hesitation in pronouncing Philip capable of any degree of cruelty and injustice, which might be necessary for the accomplishment of their destruction.

Clement was proclaimed Pope on the 5th of June, A.D. 1305. On the 14th of September, 1307, Philip, probably after previous communication with him, whom he kept in a kind of honourable captivity at Poictiers, issued circular letters to the governors of all the provinces of his kingdom, commanding them to arrest all the Templars on the 13th of October. The secret appears to have been well kept. At the dawn of day their houses were surrounded, and being wholly unprepared for resistance, they were seized and imprisoned, and their goods sequestered and inventoried.[1] The Grand Master, Jacques de Molay, had come from Cyprus with some of the knights to attend, on the invitation of the King, a conference which was to take place at Poictiers on matters of importance. They were lodged in the Temple at Paris, and were arrested there. On Sunday, October 15, Philip caused an announcement to be made in the chapel

[1] Sismondi Hist. des Français, 6, 135.

of the palace, and the other churches of Paris, of the various crimes which had caused their arrest. The Pope seems not to have expected such rapid proceedings, and he was offended that the jurisdiction, which he thought belonged to himself, should have been handed over to the archbishops, bishops, and inquisitors. The Templars had been always under the protection of the Holy See; they had immunities which were violated by the proceedings of the King. Clement therefore, by a bull dated October 27, evoked the cause to himself at Poictiers. Subsequently he so far modified his protest, that he only reserved to himself the trial of the Grand Master and the Preceptors. The prisoners were subjected to torture,[1] under which many of them expired; others confessed the crimes laid to their charge, wholly or in part. The testimony against them, on the ground of which their seizure took place, was obtained from two men of infamous lives, and that which was wrung from themselves by torture many of them subsequently retracted. The King appears to have been desirous of shifting from himself the odium of these proceedings, and called together at Tours an assembly of the nobles and third estate, before whom he laid the evidence thus obtained. The accused were not heard in their defence; the assembly adjudged them to be worthy of death. The university of Paris and the faculty of theology concurred in the sentence. Its execution is thus described by the Florentine historian,

---

[1] Dr. Lingard (Hist. 3, 472) says, "Philip on examination obtained from many a confession of the most shocking and infamous practices." He does not say "by torture."

Villani:[1] "The King caused to be erected at Saint Antoine and Saint Denys a large enclosure, surrounded by palisades, where fifty-six of the Templars were tied each to a stake, and fire applied first to their feet, then to their legs, burning them by degrees, and giving them notice at the same time, that any one of them, who would acknowledge his error and his sin, should be released from his suffering. Their friends and relations, who surrounded them in the midst of their torments, exhorted them to confess, and not suffer such disgraceful martyrdom, but none of them would make confession. On the contrary, in the midst of tears and cries, they protested that they were innocent and faithful Christians; they called Christ, Holy Mary, and the saints to their aid, and thus burnt and consumed they all expired."

Such a death renders nugatory the evidence derived from their previously extorted confession. This execution was the act of Philip alone. Subsequently, in August 1309, the Pope convoked an assembly of bishops and archbishops, who met at Paris, and before them the Grand Master, Jacques de Molay, was examined, and the confession which he was alleged to have made was read to him. He altogether denied its truth. Some of the knights repeated their former confession; others declared that it had been made under promise of pardon or threats of torture. In several places executions of the Templars took place: the order was finally dissolved at Vienne, in a Council which Clement had summoned to meet there in 1312. Great

[1] Sismondi, 6, 137.

diligence had been employed in the meantime, in collecting depositions against the Templars, and extorting confessions by the rack, if they could not otherwise be obtained. The sentence was pronounced March 6, by the Pope in a secret consistory,[1] not in the character of a judge, or on the authority of the documents in the process, which he had no legal power to do, but by way of decree[2] (provisio) and apostolic order. On the 3rd of April a second session of the Council was held; the Provision was made known to them, the order was formally abolished, and their goods transferred to the Hospitallers, "who like wrestlers of the Lord, exposing themselves unceasingly to death for the defence of the faith, incur heavy expenses in lands beyond the sea." In the following year the Grand Master and three of the commanders were brought before a commission assembled at Paris. All of them had, in their previous examinations, confessed the crimes imputed to the order. But as soon as their confessions were read, the Grand Master and the commander of Normandy revoked them. The commission would have remanded them, but Philip ordered them to be burnt that evening as relapsed heretics, and they died protesting their innocence.

[1] See the bull in Rymer, II., i., p. 5. "Ordinem Domus Militiæ Templi Jerosolymitani propter Magistrum et Fratres errorum et scelerum obscenitatibus, maculis et labe respersos (quæ propter tristem et spurcidam eorum memoriam præsentibus subticemus) non per modum diffinitivæ sententiæ, cum eam super hoc, secundum inquisitiones et processus super his habitos, non possumus ferre de jure, sed per viam provisionis, seu ordinationis Apostolicæ, irrefragabili sustulimus sanctione."

[2] Provisio, Decretum. Du Cange. The ordinances of the Oxford Parliament, A. D. 1258, are called Provisiones by the historians of the times. Dr. Lingard says, "as a measure of expediency rather than of justice;" but there is no mention of expediency in the bull. "De jure" is not *justly* but of *legal right*.

The proceedings against the Templars were so contrary to all principles of jurisprudence, that in a purely judicial point of view the evidence against them is worthless. As a question of historical probability, their partial guilt or entire innocence is not so easily settled. To the bull which Clement addressed to the English prelates, commanding them to inquire into the practices of the order, eighty-seven articles of charge are appended.[1] The same accusation is repeated in different counts, which may be condensed into the following heads.

1. That they denied the Divinity of Jesus Christ, said that he had suffered for his own crimes, and had no hope of salvation through him.

2. That those who entered the order were required to spit upon, and in various ways insult, the cross; and worshipped a cat.

3. That they did not believe in the sacrament of the altar, and that in the Canon of the Mass their priests omitted the words by which the body of Christ is made.

4. That they believed the Grand Master to have the power of giving them absolution.

5. That their receptions were clandestine, and were accompanied with indecent ceremonies.[2]

6. That they practised and allowed scandalous vices.

7. That they had heads, some with three faces, some with one, some with only a skull,

---

[1] Dugdale, Monasticon, 6, 2, 846, &c.

[2] "Deosculabantur se in ore, in ventre, in umbilico," &c.

which images they worshipped as God and their Saviour, the source of their riches and of the productions of the earth, and that they put a girdle round the forehead of the image with which they girded themselves.

8. That they imprisoned or put to death those who would not conform to the before mentioned practices, and bound all to secrecy by an oath.

9. That they swore by all means, right or wrong (per fas et nefas), to promote the increase and benefit of the order.[1]

In regard to the grossest of these imputations, nothing has come to light since the condemnation of the Templars to confirm them, so that they still rest on the original foundation of their own extorted confessions. The charge of idolatry was thought to have received confirmation from some discoveries made by the celebrated orientalist, M. Von Hammer, and published by him in his Dissertation "Mysterium Baphometis Revelatum."[2] He thought he had discovered proofs of their practice of idolatry, their Gnostic heresies, and their use of obscene images in their churches. His allegations shook the conviction of Mr. Hallam, who, in the 28th supplementary note to his Middle Ages, wavers and almost inclines to the opinion of the Templars' guilt. On the continent, however, where M. Von

---

[1] These eighty-seven counts are found in the bull *Faciens misericordiam Domini*. In another copy they are expanded to one hundred and twenty three. The only important addition is a charge of neglecting alms and hospitality. See Wilke, 2, p. 274.

[2] *Fundgruben des Orients* (Mines of the East), vol. 6, 1. Baphomet is a corrupted form of Mahomet, to whom the Templars were alleged to do homage.

Hammer thought he had found in sculptures, paintings, and mediæval objects,[1] the evidences of their heresies and vicious practices, his proofs are considered arbitrary and fanciful; and so they are regarded by Dean Milman, who has fully examined the question in the fifth volume of his History of Latin Christianity. The ninth charge is an adversary's invidious statement of a principle of action, which belongs to most incorporated bodies, but is strenuously denied by all. The charge of unsoundness in the faith has more probability than that of idolatry, and the insulting renunciation of Christianity. An under-current of free-thinking on religious subjects pervades society, while all at the surface appears to be acquiescence and unanimity; and the more it is denied outward expression by legitimate channels, the more strongly it is manifested in those secret associations, in which men can unbosom themselves without fear. It is not likely, indeed, that warriors, who could neither write nor read, would trouble themselves with the subtilties of Gnosticism; but they had learned clerks among them who might indulge themselves in heretical speculations which they durst not avow in public, and the layman might ridicule as an absurdity the doctrine which the priest inculcated as a mystery. To us it may seem that men who took the cross and left their homes for a foreign land, must have been animated by a spirit of piety,

---

[1] Certain jettons, assigned by Von Hammer to the Templars, and considered to exhibit their impious symbols, Mr. King (Ancient Gems, p. 352) says are the bracteate coins of German Margraves. Many churches contain indecent sculptures, but the proof that they belonged exclusively to the Templars entirely fails.

which would keep them at the greatest possible distance from everything profane; but after the first impulse of enthusiasm in the foundation of the order had spent itself, the love of the profession of arms and the dignity of knighthood, the fellowship of distinguished men, a share in the possessions of a wealthy order, had probably more to do in recruiting the ranks of the Templars than religious zeal. We may think that pious feeling would be exalted and faith confirmed by residence in

> "——— Those holy fields
> Over whose acres walked those blessed feet,
> Which fourteen hundred years ago were nailed
> For our advantage to the bloody cross."
> *Henry IV.*, 1., i.

But the contrary effect seems to be produced; the resident views with indifference that which excites the enthusiasm of the pilgrim. The piety of Dr. Johnson might grow warmer amidst the ruins of Iona; the inhabitants care little about St. Columba, or the blessings which his missionaries diffused among the roving barbarians.

Even the parodies of the services and ceremonies of the church imputed to the Templars, if true, will appear less atrocious, when we consider how irreverently they were sometimes treated by churchmen themselves, as in the Feast of the Innocents, or the Feast of Fools, and the mock ceremony of the Boy-Bishop;[1] or the Feast of the Ass at

---

[1] See on this subject Gregorie, Episcopus Puerorum. There was at Salisbury a monument to a boy-bishop. Du Cange, Kalendæ, quotes an inventory of the Cathedral of York, taken in 1530, in which mention is made of a mitre for the boy-bishop.

Beauvais,[1] where an ass was led in procession to the altar, and an imitation of his bray by the priest was substituted for the *Amen* at the end of the Mass, the people braying in response. These things were condemned by the Councils of the Church, but they were practised in churches and even in cathedral churches. The public ceremonies of initiation into the order were grave and dignified, but it is said that they were parodied by blasphemous and indecent proceedings. Some recent extraordinary revelations of courts martial (1856) prove what a disposition there is in young military men, to play off coarse practical jokes on new-comers. And if such things are done amidst the refinement of the nineteenth century, what may we not believe of the grosser manners of the thirteenth? It is very possible that the kiss of reception into the order may have been parodied, in those extraordinary *oscula* before referred to.[2]

That many of the Templars were stained with the licentiousness of the age is by no means improbable. St. Bernard miscalculated the efficacy of vows and discipline, when he endeavoured to exact, from high-spirited youthful warriors, virtues not always easy even to a macerated monk. Gallantry was the soul of chivalry, and probably many a Templar regarded his vow as only a prohibition of marriage. Profligacy was but too characteristic

---

[1] Rigollot, Monnaies des Fous, p. 31; Wright, Archæological Album; Du Cange, Festum Asini. He concludes his account of the ceremonies with the words, "Hæc ægre retulimus, quippe quæ theatro magis quam ecclesiasticæ cæremoniæ conveniant." The idea, however, appears to have been originally religious, the ass being the representative of that which carried the Virgin into Egypt.

[2] See note on p. 35.

of the age; it may well have been rife among the Templars, when it had taken such root among ecclesiastics and monks.[1] The enormities imputed, and with apparent justice, to Boniface VIII., equalled or exceeded those which were alleged against the Templars. And if it should be said that they were calumnies in the case of the Pope, it may be replied, that the evidence was less suspicious than that on which the Templars were condemned. On this point we may do justice to the motives of Philip. He was a monarch of grave character and strict morality, and his horror of the loose lives of the Templars was probably sincere. It was with great difficulty that Clement dissuaded him from insisting that the memory of Boniface should be branded with infamy. The order of the Templars may have been made a scape-goat for the Holy See.

I am the more inclined to believe that Philip was sincere in his conviction that morality demanded the suppression of the Templars, from the pains which he took to procure its extension to the other kingdoms of Europe. He had no personal interest in their suppression in England, but he wrote to Edward II., charging them with horrible crimes, and sent an agent to enforce his request for their seizure. The proceedings of Edward are remarkable. He wrote in answer to Philip, that he had laid the matter before the Council, but that the charges seemed to them and him incredible. As

---

[1] The chapter *De Vita et Honestate Clericorum*, in the Constitut. Synod. Winton. (Wilkins, 2, 296), gives no flattering picture of the morals of the clergy.

however some of the scandals were alleged to have occurred in Guienne, an English province, he would summon the Seneschal of Agen to his presence. The result of this interview, which was to take place at Boulogne,[1] is not told us, but he wrote on the 4th of December, 1307, to the Kings of Portugal, Castille and Leon, Arragon, and Sicily, exhorting them to allow nothing to be done against those who had exhibited devotion to the church, and defended it in foreign countries, upon mere rumour, without legal conviction.[2] To the Pope at the same time he wrote, highly praising the Templars for their good conduct, and exhorting him to institute proceedings by which their conduct might be cleared.[3] Meanwhile he so far conformed to the policy of Philip, that in January 1308[4] the property of the Templars and the persons of many of them were seized by his orders. His change of feeling towards them had been produced by a letter from the Pope, informing him of the discoveries made by Philip's inquisitions; he may have also been desirous of courting Philip's favour. For at that time he was on the point of proceeding to Boulogne, to receive the hand of Philip's daughter, Isabella, "the she-wolf of France," to whom he owed many of the misfortunes of his life and his horrible death.

The bull "Faciens misericordiam," issued from Poictiers on the 12th of August, 1309, in which the Pope relates the measures taken to inquire into the truth of the charges against the Templars, and

[1] Rymer, 3, 32, Nov. 26th.
[2] Rymer, Dec. 4th.
[3] Rymer, Dec. 10th.
[4] Rymer, 3, 34. The order applied to the three kingdoms, but it was provided that the Templars should not be kept "in dura et vili prisona."

to which the eighty-seven articles are appended which had resulted from the investigation, reached the Archbishop of Canterbury in September 1309. He transmitted it, and the accompanying documents, to his suffragans on the 22nd of September, and, in obedience to his mandate, the Bishop of London forthwith ordered that all the Templars in the city and diocese of London should, on the following Sunday after mass, be cited to appear before him. Two French ecclesiastics had been sent over in the preceding month, appointed by the Pope to preside at the trials. The imprisoned Templars were at the same time ordered to be brought from the Southern Counties to London, from the Midland to Lincoln, and from the Northern to York. The examinations in London produced no evidence in support of the charges contained in the Pope's bull. He was dissatisfied that torture had not been used, and the weak monarch gave way and ordered the application of torture, provided it did not extend to the shedding of blood or mutilation of the body. This power was used; but besides the rack every method was taken to harass and exhaust the prisoners, so as to drive them to confession. All that could be obtained from them by repeated interrogatories was only hearsay, and the testimony against them, tendered by those who did not belong to the order, came from the most polluted sources. They put in a solemn declaration of their innocence and their orthodoxy, appealed to those among whom they had lived, and declared their readiness to submit to censure and punishment if, in their ignorance, they had said or done anything wrong.

It is an affecting document, and no one can read it without being convinced, that whatever may have been the levity or the vice of individuals, the order was free from all serious imputation. At length two apostates, Stephen de Stapelbrigg and Thomas de Thoroldby, both serving brothers, were induced to confess to the spitting on the cross, and the denial of the divinity of Christ; and a chaplain of the order, John de Stoke, deposed, that on his admission into the order by Jacques de Molay, the Grand Master, a crucifix was exhibited to him, and he was told to deny the Saviour who was represented upon it, which he did through fear of death. Hereupon Stapelbrigg and Thoroldsby were brought before the Ecclesiastical Commissioners, and having adhered to their confession, and affixed their mark (for they could not read), they received absolution, and were re-admitted into the Church. John de Stoke was absolved and re-admitted in the same way. From the rest no other confession could be obtained, than that they had been guilty in receiving absolution from the Master of the Temple, who, as a layman, had no power to grant it.[1] Upon signing a declaration to this effect, along with a vague and general confession, that they could not purge themselves of the heresies set forth under the apostolic bull, they were reconciled to the

---

[1] The form in which the Master or his deputy dissolved a Chapter is given in French among the examinations of the Scotch Templars (Wilkins, 2, 383). No pardon would be granted for embezzling the alms of the house, or keeping any property to himself; but of the sins which they had not confessed, "pour honte de la chair ou pour peur de la justice de la mesoun," he absolved them by virtue of the power which the Pope had given him.

Church at the south door of St. Paul's. Many of those confined in the Tower were too feeble or too ill to bear removal, and were absolved and reconciled at St. Mary's Chapel, near the Tower.[1]

It has been already related (p. 41) that in January 1308 orders had been given, that the Templars throughout England should be arrested and their property sequestered. The King had sent a writ to the Sheriff of Yorkshire, Sir John de Creppinge, commanding him to summon twenty-four discreet and faithful knights, to be at York on the morrow of the Purification, the day appointed for the capture of the Templars. In their presence he was to open the sealed orders, in the execution of which they were to assist. The motive of this secrecy is obvious; it was desirable not only to seize the persons of the Templars, but to prevent concealment or colourable transfer of their property. The order is endorsed with a return of the proceedings. The Templars were placed in custody in various parts of the county. On the 4th of March, 1309, an order in the French language is issued to those who had them in charge in the province of York, to bring them to York, and produce them before the Abbat of Lagny and Sicard de Vaur, the Pope's chaplain and auditor of causes, two of the Commissioners appointed by the Pope to conduct the inquiry, and allow them to be dealt with according to ecclesiastical law.[2] At the same time the King of France addressed a letter to Archbishop Green-

---

[1] See the account of the proceedings in London, in Addison, chap. x.

[2] Rymer, 3, 34, 43, 202.

field, strongly urging his co-operation.[1] The matter could not be strange to the Archbishop. He had received consecration from Clement V. at Lyons in the beginning of the year 1307, in which the Templars were arrested throughout France, and the character both of the Pope and Philip must have been well known to him. On the 11th of March, 1309-10, he issued from London his summons to a provincial Council, to meet at York on the 20th of May, 1310. Meanwhile the Ecclesiastical Commissioners had not been idle in preparing evidence for the Council. The Templars, who had been brought together from all the northern counties to York, had undergone examination from April 27th to the 4th of May. We are surprised to find that they were only twenty-five in number. Most of their names indicate their Yorkshire origin.[2] Among them were the preceptor of Ribston, William de Grafton; the preceptor of Faxfleet, William de la Fenne; the preceptor of Newsham, Godfrey de Arches, and two priests. William de Grafton, as appears from his examination, had been thirty-two years in the order, having been admitted in London by the Grand Master. Being questioned on the subject of its imputed heresies he replied, that he believed as other men believed, and as to the abnegation of Christ, charged in the articles 73—77, he declared that he had never heard of such things. The examination of the Templars in France had been

[1] Raine's Fasti Eboracenses, p. 371.
[2] The names of Stamford, Kerby, Bellerby, Langton, Roucliff, Wylton, Ripon, Thresk, Shefeld, Eberston, Midelton, Clifton, all represent places in Yorkshire whence the patronymic was derived. See the entire list in Fasti Eboracenses, p. 372.

proceeding, and, by the means already described, (p. 31), confessions of atrocious crimes had been wrung from them. He was reminded of these, but declared that if they had really made them, they had lied. Thomas de Stamford, who had been admitted in Cyprus, deposed that the Grand Preceptor, a knight, or the Visitor, could absolve from the seven deadly sins, if the offender implored mercy from the Chapter and did penance; and that he needed no absolution from a priest, unless the Preceptor commanded him to consult one.[1] The preceptors of Newsham and Faxfleet and several of the knights were examined, touching the ceremonies of initiation and the power of absolution, but nothing of a criminal character was elicited from them. Matter of graver accusation against the Yorkshire Templars had meanwhile been obtained by means of the inquisitorial proceedings carried on in London.[2] John de Nassington had said, that Milo de Stapleton and Adam de Everingham had told him, that they had once been invited by the Grand Preceptor of Yorkshire to a great feast at Temple-Hurst, and that they had been told them (it is not said by whom) that the knights assembled there to worship a calf. John de Eure, Sheriff of Yorkshire, said, that before the seizure of the Templars, and before any scandal

---

[1] "Interrogatus de quibus remittuntur ad sacerdotes, dicit, quod de occulto lapsu carnis et de aliis absolvit sacerdos, quando veniunt ad eum, excepta Simonia." Wilkins, 2, p. 372.

[2] Fasti Eboracenses, p. 371, where some important additions are made, from the Register of Archbishop Greenfield, to the account of the proceedings in Wilkins' Concilia. Mr. Raine observes how bitter was the hostility of the Mendicants to the Templars. The Templars were the aristocrats, the Mendicants the plebeians.

respecting them was in circulation, William de la Fenne, preceptor of Westerdale, had been invited to his house, and that after dinner he took a book from his bosom and gave it to the sheriff's lady. She, who must have far surpassed most of her sex in that age, both in letters and theology, found in it a paper containing very heretical propositions concerning Christ and the Christian faith. She handed it to her husband who, when he had read it, questioned the preceptor about its contents. William de la Fenne smiled, and said the man who wrote it was a great ribald, but would not part with the book. William de la Forde, rector of Crofton, swore that a deceased priest of the Augustine order had told him that Patrick de Rippon, a Templar, had revealed to him in confession that the knights were guilty of horrid blasphemies and crimes. Being questioned when he had heard these things, he said, in the city of York, since the seizure of the Templars. Robert de Oteringham, a Minorite, swore, that after returning thanks the chaplain of Ribston rebuked the brethren, and told them that the devil would burn them, or words to that effect. The threat was not undeserved, if his subsequent account of the indecencies committed by them were true. One circumstance deposed to by this witness shows, how ready the enemies of the Templars were to seize on anything, which could be made the ground of accusation against them.[1] He had seen at Ribston a crucifix laid upon an altar, and said to a Templar that it was disrespectfully placed, and should be

[1] Wilkins, 2, p. 398.

raised up; to which the Templar replied, "Put the cross down, and leave it in peace." Twenty years before, when he was at Wetherby, he was told the Grand Preceptor, who happened to be there, did not come to table, because he was preparing an exhibition of some relics which he had brought from the Holy Land. He heard in the night a noise in the chapel, and getting up looked through the keyhole, and saw—a great light from a fire or candle! Next morning when he asked one of the Templars what saint's festival they had been keeping, he turned very pale and charged him, as he valued his life, not to say a word of what he had seen.[1] Such hearsays would never be received in evidence by any court of law, but they contributed their share to bring odium on the Templars, and prepare their ecclesiastical judges for their condemnation.

Before the second Council met, the Templars, who in the meantime had been in York Castle, were brought up to the Chapter House; the previous proceedings and depositions were explained to the audience in their mother tongue, and the Templars put in a paper in the French language, along with certain papal bulls relating to their

---

[1] A story something similar was told by Gasper de Nafferton, who had been at Ribston when William de Pocklington was admitted by William de Grafton, preceptor of Ribston. The knights had held a meeting in the night with closed doors. Some one had bargained with the doorkeeper for two shillings to be admitted to the ceremony, but the doorkeeper had not kept his word, and he was told that if he had seen what went on, he must either have entered the order or been put to death. He also deposed that a cross, which had been left standing the night before, was found on the ground. These things excited no suspicion at the time, but after the infamy of the Templars was made known, the chaplain "concepit sinistram suspicionem ex his." Wilkins, 2, 363.

order. Being again brought up on a subsequent day, their answers were reduced to writing by the notaries,[1] and the following Friday was fixed for the final decision. But a further deliberation was found necessary. The Archbishop was at this time probably intending to visit the Nottinghamshire portion of his diocese. He therefore appointed the Council to be held in the conventual church of Blyth;[2] but changed his mind, and it was actually held at York on the 1st of July.

The assemblage of churchmen in the Minster on that day must have been very imposing.[3] The Archbishop was seated on his tribunal, attended by his Suffragans, the bishops of Durham and Whithern (Casa Candida) in Galloway; the Dean of York and of the prebendal churches of Aukland and Lancaster; the Archdeacon of Cleveland, the Chancellor of the church of York, Doctor in Theology; the Abbats of St. Mary's, York, Kirkstall, Roche, Rievaulx, Meaux, Fountains, Rufford (Notts.), Furness, Calder, Cokersand, Jorvaulx, St. Agatha (Easby), Egleston, Newminster; the Priors of Holy Trinity and St. Andrew, York, of St. Oswyth Pontefract, of Drax, Bretton, Guisborough, Newburgh, Malton, Marton, Gronmis (Grosmont?), Thurgarton, Felseye (Felly, Notts.), Mattersey, Blyth, Bridlington, Kirkholm (Kirkham), Warter, Ellerton; Thomas de Clifford, John Gower, Philip of Beverley, Doctors in Theology; the Friars Geffrey of Haxby, a monk

---

[1] Wilkins, 2, 397.
[2] Wilkins, 2, 358.
[3] The proceedings are said to have taken place "in capitulo." The age of the Chapter-House is uncertain, but it can hardly in 1311 have attained the superlative beauty which it claims in the well known line "Ut rosa phlos phlorum, sic est domus ista domorum."

of Durham, Adam de Lincoln, a Minorite of York, Thomas de Pontefract, of the same order, Richard de Wetwang, an Augustinian of York, Thomas de Midelton, a Friar Preacher; Nicolas of Oxford, Richard of Chester, and Robert of Sancthorpe, Professors of Canon Law. All these personally appeared; a multitude of ecclesiastical personages were represented by their procurators.

The Archbishop took for his text Acts iv. 32: "And the multitude of them that believed was of one heart and of one mind." This unanimity, however, did not at first prevail; for the Templars having been brought up and afterwards removed, along with all the clergy and laity who had not been summoned to the Council, "great disputation and continued altercation arose between the aforesaid doctors, professors, and dignitaries, upon the reasons and motives touching the business of the Templars and the Templars themselves." Ultimately the business was adjourned to the next day, when a committee was appointed, consisting of doctors and professors of the canon law, and other discreet and learned persons, more fully to treat of and deliberate upon the matter, and report to the Archbishop on the following Monday. When Monday arrived, much further discussion took place, and the Archbishop appointed a committee to draw up a memorial to be presented to the Pope, which was to be laid before the Council on the following Saturday, with liberty to the Templars to controvert it if they thought expedient. On Saturday, the 10th of July, Robert de Pickering, the Archbishop's Commissary, presiding, the matter was again handled, the Archbishop himself being absent and not appearing at any subsequent stage of the proceedings. A further adjournment took place to Wednesday in the following week, the 28th of July. The attendance had at this time much diminished; only the Bishop of Whithern, the Dean of York, the Chancellor of the Church, the Archdeacon of Cleveland, the Abbats of St. Mary's, Kirkstall, Selby, Jorvaulx, Roche, Meaux, Coverham, Egleston, Rievaulx, Byland; the Priors of the Holy Trinity, St. Andrew, Pontefract, and Drax, were present. An adjournment to next day took place, that the absent members might make their appearance. We find, however, no further mention of them.

On the 29th of July, the twenty-four Templars, with William de Grafton at their head, appeared before the Commissary and the other ecclesiastical dignitaries, and all and singular of them, each for himself confessed and distinctly acknowledged, and that of his own free will, that there had been very scandalous reports concerning them (se vehementer diffamatos fuisse) in regard to the articles contained in the papal bulls, and that they could not clear themselves (de eisdem non posse se purgare), and all and every one on his knees humbly prayed that they might be re-admitted to the Church (statum ecclesiæ sibi concedi), affirming that they were ready in all things to conform to the orders of the Church respecting the premises. Then each of them, touching the Holy Evangelists, took the following oath in his mother tongue: "I, *A. B.*, detest and abjure on these Holy Evangelists all heresies, and especially those contained in the papal bull, and promise in all other matters to keep the Catholic and orthodox faith, which the Holy Roman Church holds, teaches, and preaches. So help me God and these his Evangelists." Having taken this oath, they proceeded immediately to the South door of the Minster, and swore to obey all the commands of the Church. Thereupon the Bishop of Whithern, in his pontifical robes, the Dean and Chancellor of the Church, the Archdeacon of Cleveland, and the Abbat of St. Mary's standing by, absolved them from all the heresies contained in the papal bull, and from all others, and restored them to the Church and to its sacraments. The Templars then returned to the Chapter House, where Robert de Pickering released them from the King's custody and prison, and admitted them to the custody of the Church. The Council was adjourned to the following day, the 30th of July, and the eleventh of its sitting, when the Commissary pronounced that they should be distributed among the monasteries of the diocese to perform penance, the mode and form of which should be prescribed by the Archbishop and his colleagues. The Council then adjourned *sine die*.

Considering the whole of these proceedings, I can come to no other conclusion, than that the Templars, having the fate of their brethren in France and in the South before their eyes, had consented to that modified confession which their words involve, on condition that their lives should be spared. Its expressions are remarkable. They do not plead guilty to the charges of the papal bull, which they could not have done without accusing themselves of falsehood in their examinations; they only say that they cannot clear themselves. Their oath of abjuration is not a confession of heresy, any more than the abjuration of the Pretender in an oath of allegiance was a confession of having been a Jacobite. To abjure is to repudiate, not necessarily to renounce, under the sanction of an oath. Mr. Raine justly observes, that the proceeding was, on the whole, creditable to the northern clergy. The praise of abstaining from torture belongs rather to the civil authorities, in whose custody the prisoners were.

The distribution of the Templars among the monasteries soon took place.[1] John de Nassington, whose name has been already mentioned as deposing to an idle story against them (p. 46), was appointed their penancer,[2] and before a twelvemonth had passed their sentence of excommunication was taken off. This mode of disposing of them is a strong evidence that the archbishop did not believe the more serious charges against them. If he had thought them to be, in the language of the papal bull, "non tam nefandis quam infandis errorum et scelerum obscenitatibus, maculis et labe respersos," would he have run the risk of corrupting the monasteries of his diocese, by introducing such a mass of pollution into them? Nothing in the conduct of the Templars, while relegated to the monasteries, justified[3] the imputations against them. Pensions of four-pence a day were granted to them from their sequestered estates, or from those which

---

[1] See the particulars in Fasti Eboracenses, p. 375, note *b*.
[2] Fasti, p. 374, note *y*.
[3] Ibid., note *d*.

were transferred to the Hospitallers.[1] In the south they appear to have fared worse. Many of them put on the garments of laymen; some married wives; others wandered about the country in such forlorn guise, letting their beards grow long, that Edward II. had to protect his valet who was going to travel, by special letters, that his long beard might not lead to his being taken for a fugitive Templar.[2]

The Council of Vienne was not sitting, and the formal sentence of annullation had not been pronounced, when these proceedings took place at York, but it had been adjourned to the 1st of October, 1311. Archbishop Greenfield had been invited to take a part in it. He proceeded to Vienne in the course of that month, and was treated, as his historian Stubbs informs us, with marked distinction. The proceedings of the Council on the 22nd of March, 1312, have already been described. Greenfield, who had returned to England, after being present at the formal dissolution of the order pronounced in April of that year, published from Cawood, on the 14th of August, a decree in which he declared it for ever abolished, and forbade anyone, under pain of the greater excommunication, from entering the order, or wearing its habit, or in any way behaving himself as a Templar. That they might not pretend ignorance, the decree was

---

[1] Larking, p. 137. John de Hoperton, formerly a Templar, appears as enjoying a corrody, i.e., free maintenance, from the preceptory of Wetherby, then held by the Hospitallers. Among the charges on their revenues in 1338 are the *vadia* or annual wages, six marks each, of twelve Templars, among whom are several Yorkshiremen.

[2] Addison, p. 579.

to be published in the Cathedral of York, and all other churches, collegiate, conventual, and parochial, throughout the diocese.[1] So ends the history of the order of Templars in Yorkshire.[2]

The records of the Exchequer contain numerous documents relating to the property of the Templars in this county. There are inventories of all the stock and furniture found on their manors of Allerthorpe, Brompton, Newsome, Whitby, Etton, Westerdale, Wetherby and Sicklinghall, Copmanthorpe, Faxfleet, Foukbrigg (Foulbridge near Yeddingham), Ribston, Cowton, and Hurst. Specimens of these have been printed from the public records, in the Gentleman's Magazine, 1857, pt. 2, p. 519, including the Castle Mills at York, Copmanthorpe, Temple Newsome, and Temple Hurst, all of which places were visited and their contents scheduled, if we may believe the date of the return, on a single winter's day, Dec. 1, 1311. These properties had been in the hands of Adam de Hoperton, as custo-

---

[1] Wilkins, Concilia, 2, 401.

[2] It may be interesting to read some opinions respecting the dissolution of the order. The Dominican who passes by the name of Stubbs, and who probably wrote soon after the death of Thoresby, (1373) since he does not mention his successor, Arbp. Neville, says, "Præsentibus ipsis Templariis, et ad omnia eis objecta per æmulos suos respondentibus, quamvis in multis essent accusati nihil tamen inventum est quod de jure videretur statum illorum anuullare." Our Yorkshire historian, Walter of Hemingbrough, says, "Erant pro ordine Templariorum prælati quasi omnes, præter prælatos Franciæ, qui propter timorem regis Franciæ per quem, ut dicebatur, totum illud scandalum fuerat, aliud facere non audebant." The Scottish historian Spotiswood says of the Templars, "The rumour went, that Philip, King of France, to get one of his sons made King of Jerusalem and possessed of their revenues, did labour to have them and their order condemned. But howsoever their destruction was wrought, all authors testify, that notwithstanding the cruel torments which divers of them were put unto, none of the crimes laid to their charge could ever be made out against them." P. 51.

dian, since the seizure of the Templars' goods, and were now delivered over to Alexander de Cave and Robert de Amcotes. The chapel at the Castle Mills appears to have been well furnished with books, vestments, and vessels, and it is noted that the chalice had been valued at a hundred shillings,[1] when the Templars were seized, but that it was not worth so much. The inventory is most minute, including even a cracked pan, *patellam debilem*. Thence the Commissioners proceeded to Copmanthorpe. The prices of the produce found on the manors may be worth recording; "mixtilis" (maslin), 3s. 4d. a quarter; oats, 2s.; wheat (frumentum), 4s.; peas, 2s. 6d.; a cart horse (equus carectarius), 11s.; a plough horse (affrus pro carucis), 5s.; a plough ox, 10s.; a cow, 6s. 8d.; a goose (auca), 3d. From other valuations we learn that the price of a boar was 4s.; of a sow, 20d.; of a ewe, 12d.; of a wether (multo), 15d.; a lamb, 8d.; an ass, 3s. The return of stock from Newsome shows the magnitude of the establishment. There were forty-four plough oxen, fourteen plough horses, four hundred and fifty-four sheep, three hundred and thirty-five wethers, one hundred and forty-seven lambs. The tithe of Whitkirk, which was in sheaf, is valued at 50 marks. Temple Hurst was inferior to Newsome in live stock, but had a large acreage in crops of grain. In both establishments the

---

[1] Edward II. was in York in the winter of 1311 and spring of 1312, and by a grant "teste me ipso apud Eboracum xxx die Maii anno regni nostri quinto," he increased the salary of the chaplain at the Castle Mills from six marks to eight. Edward had come to York to meet Gaveston, had retired to Newcastle on the approach of the Earl of Lancaster, and returning by sea to Scarborough, had come back to York in the beginning of May.

kitchen appears to have been well furnished with pans, pots, frying pans, tripods, mortars, gridirons, pickling tubs, and a brewing apparatus. Temple Hurst, standing near the Aire, had boats and nets for fishing. With the exception of a sacramental cup, which appears in all the valuations, there is no mention of plate. The kitchen at Newsome contained three mazer bowls[1] (ciphi murrei), valued at 2s. each. All arms and military equipments would no doubt be taken possession of when the Templars were arrested.

The spoliation of the order had been accomplished by a combination between the Pope and the sovereigns of Europe, aided by the aristocracy, who hoped to recover what their ancestors had given away. The division of the spoil was not so easy. The Pope would gladly have transferred their property to the Hospitallers, who were now the only military body devoted to the defence of Christendom, and who had raised their reputation by their seizure of the island of Rhodes, and their gallant resistance to the Turks. But it was far from the intention of the secular powers to raise up a second military order, and endow it with the means of becoming troublesome to the state. The selfishness of the sovereigns and the nobles soon betrayed itself. Both Edward II. and Philip of France showed themselves well disposed to have kept the goods of the Templars in their own hands, if the Pope had not interposed and urged them

---

[1] Of these mazer bowls, see a paper by Robert Davies, Esq., and Albert Way, Esq., in the Proceedings of Arch. Institute, York, 1846, p. 24.

to bestow them on the Hospitallers. The king and the lords of the fees granted to the Templars were very unwilling to yield them to the Hospitallers. The question had been formally proposed to the Council, including the king's justices, whether the lords of the fees or others, who had taken possession of the tenements of the Templars, could retain them, "secundum legem terræ et sana conscientia," according to the law of the land, and with a safe conscience. They answered that they might by the law of the land; the question of conscience they did not decide. Parliament interposed, and by an Act passed in the 17th year of Edward II.'s reign (1324)[1] it was declared, that inasmuch as the lands had been given for the defence of Christianity against the Saracens and other enemies of Christ, neither the king nor the lords of the fees could hold the Templars' lands, and that no donation or inheritance since the Dissolution could be pleaded. But as the Knights Hospitallers had been instituted for the same pious purposes, it was enacted that they should have the Templars' lands, subject to all the pensions, hospitalities, and obligations, to which they had been subject while held by the Templars. The statute concludes by empowering them to recover anything to which they were entitled.

This restitution after all was very imperfectly made. The lately published volume of "The Hospitallers in England" shows what difficulty they had in getting possession. In 1338, when this Survey was made, they had in Yorkshire Whitley,

---

[1] Ruffhead's Statutes at Large, Appendix, p. 23.

Etton, Foukbrigg, Alverthorpe, Westerdale and Copmanthorpe, Cowton, Ribston, and Wetherby;[1] but the rich manors of Temple Hurst and Temple Newsom, with Faxfleet, Carlton, and Normanton, were in other hands.[2] The Crown had appropriated the Castle Mills at York; Temple Hurst and Temple Newsome had been given to the Countess of Pembroke, Faxfleet to Ralph Neville, Carlton to Hugh le Despencer, Normanton to Lord de Roos. Some of those which were in their hands had probably suffered waste from the lords of the fee, as those in other counties had.[3] Aymer de Valence, Earl of Pembroke, held the Temple in London during his life. At his death it was transferred to the Hospitallers, who leased it to the Students of the Law,[4] and built themselves the Priory of St. John's, Clerkenwell, the remains of which form the frontispiece to the pages of the immortal Sylvanus Urban.

To trace the history of the properties once belonging to this order in Yorkshire, requires a knowledge of topography and genealogy to which I make no pretension. By inquiries in all the localities mentioned in their history much knowledge might yet be obtained. I subjoin to this paper a list made out by Mr. W. H. Black of all the documents connected with the Suppression,

---

[1] Larking, p. 212.
[2] Mr. Larking considers "Normanton le Vale" to be Temple Normanton in Derbyshire; but I think it more probable that it is the Yorkshire Normanton, in the vale of the Calder, well known to railway travellers.
[3] Larking, p. 133, 172, 183.
[4] "And so," says Fuller, "these buildings are turned to better purpose, these new Templars defending one Christian from another, as the old ones defended Christians from Pagans."

lately in the Carlton Ride branch of the Public Record Office, and now transferred to the General Record Office. They may assist in local investigations. If another JOSEPH HUNTER should ever arise, to write the history of the North and East Ridings, as the history of South Yorkshire has been written by him, the descent of the Templars' and Hospitallers' lands will be accurately traced. I shall only mention the disposal of a few of their principal preceptories.

Ribston, which was transferred to the Hospitallers, was granted, when they in their turn were dissolved, to the Duke of Suffolk, and sold by him to Henry Goodricke, brother of Thomas Goodricke, Bishop of Ely and Lord Chancellor in the reign of Edward VI. By the will of the last heir male of the Goodrickes it passed to Sir Francis Holyoake, and is now in the possession of John Dent, Esq.

Temple Newsome and Temple Hurst were granted by agreement with the Hospitallers[1] to the Countess of Pembroke for life, and after her death by Edward III. to Sir J. D'Arcy. His descendant in the reign of Henry VIII. took part in the Pilgrimage of Grace, and was beheaded in London in 1537. Temple Newsome, having been forfeited to the Crown, was granted by Henry VIII. in 1544, to Lord Lennox and the Lady Margaret his wife. Their son, the unfortunate Darnley, was born there. Being again united to the Crown, it was granted by James I. to his cousin, Esme Stuart, second Duke of Lennox and Richmond, who had married the only daughter and heiress of Sir Henry

[1] Thoresby's Ducatus, p. 226.

D'Arcie of Brimham. His extravagance led to its alienation, and Temple Newsome became the property of Sir Arthur Ingram, whose father, Hugh Ingram, a native of Thorp-on-the-Hill near Wakefield, was a wealthy London draper. Sir Arthur himself was a person of high consideration, a member and secretary of the Council of the North, high sheriff of this county, and representative of the city of York in the last parliament of James I. and the two first of Charles I. He built himself a splendid house, with gardens extending to the city wall, near the north-west end of the Minster, where Charles I. was lodged in 1642, and of which some remains were to be seen a few years since.[1] By his marriage with a daughter of Lord Fairfax of Gilling, and his son's with a daughter of Lord Fauconberg, he became allied to the aristocracy of the county. His second son was rewarded by Charles II. for his adherence to the royal cause, with the Scottish Viscounty of Irwin. By marriage with a daughter of the ninth Viscount, Temple Newsome came to the Marquis of Hertford, who took the name of Ingram, and at his son's death to the representative of the family of Meynell, whose ancestor had married the third daughter of the ninth Viscount Irwin.

Sir Arthur Ingram entirely rebuilt Temple Newsome, and though the apartment is still pointed out

---

[1] Drake, p. 370, 357, 354. Cave's Antiquities of York, pl. xi. The Duke and Duchess of York took up their abode there in 1666, when they came into the north to avoid the plague then raging in London. Drake, 175. York contained other memorials of Sir Arthur. He founded by his will the hospital in Bootham, and gave to the Minster three of the chandeliers by which the choir used to be lighted.

in which Darnley was born, there is no proof that any part of the original house of the Templars remains. Thoresby¹ speaks of a bed, which apparently had formed part of the furniture of the former house, inscribed in gold letters, *Avant Darnley Jamais Derrière*. When Sir Arthur rebuilt the house he placed, according to the pious custom of the times, the following inscription in stone work on the walls. ALL GLORY AND PRAISE TO GOD THE FATHER, THE SON, AND THE HOLY GHOST ON HIGH, PEACE, GOOD WILL TOWARD MEN, HONOUR AND TRUE ALLEGIANCE TO OUR GRACIOUS KING, LOVING AFFECTIONS AMONGST HIS SUBJECTS, HEALTH AND PLENTY WITHIN THIS HOUSE.² The town of Leeds still retains traces of the ancient privileges of the Templars of Newsome, some houses, which had belonged to them, being marked with their cross, as a sign of exemption from the obligation to grind at the Soke mill. Timble-Bridge, leading from Leeds to Newsome, is said by Thoresby³ to be a corruption of Temple-Bridge. Temple Hurst, not having become the residence of any wealthy family, has escaped being modernized, and still retains a considerable part of the Templars' buildings.

---

[1] Ducatus Leodiensis, p. 226.
[2] Dr. Whitaker, Loidis and Elmete, p. 133, speaks mysteriously of a cup, found since Thoresby's time, which he refers to the Templars, but does not explain the evidence on which he relies.
[3] Ducatus, p. 99.

APPENDIX OF DOCUMENTS.

Documents of the reign of Edward II., relating to the Templars of Yorkshire, among the Records of the Remembrancer of the Exchequer, in the Public Record Office, London.

First, a bundle marked "T. G., 41156," containing several files of documents, and some loose.

First File.

No. 1. Writ commanding the Sheriff of Yorkshire to attach all the Templars in his bailiwick, seize all their lands and goods, together with their charters, writings, and muniments, make an inventory thereof, till their lands, keep their bodies in safe custody; and certify the Treasurer and Barons of the Exchequer of his proceedings. (Dated at Byflete, 20th Dec., 1 E. 2.) Indorsed with a return of his proceedings.

No. 2. Indenture on behalf of Sir John de Creppinge, Sheriff of Yorkshire, between Sir John Dayrill and John de Walden, keeper of the manor of Cave, stating all the corn sold at Cave, and the cattle and goods found there. (Wednesday after Epiphany, 1 E. 2.)

No. 3. Inventory made in the manor of Alwarthorp. (Same date.)

No. 4. The like at Penhill. (Same date.)

No. 5. ———— Brampton. „

No. 6. ———— the Chapel of the Templars of York; "ornaments" and furniture only. (Same date.)

No. 7. The like at Neusom. „

No. 8. ———— Wythele. „

No. 9. ———— Etton. „

No. 10. ———— Westerdale. „

No. 11. ———— Wetherby and Sikklinghale. (Same date.)

No. 12. ———— Coupemanthorpe. (Same date.)

No. 13. ———— Faxflete. „

No. 14. ———— Foukbrigg, Alnestan (Allerston ?), and Wyddale. (Same date.)

No. 15. The like at Rybbestan. (Same date.)
No. 16. ———— Couton, or Temple-Couton. (Same date.)
No. 17. ———— Hyrst. (Same date.)
No. 2—17 appear to be Transcripts only.

Original Inquisition relative to a grant of corrody, claimed by William Const of Ireland, out of the House of the Temple of Hyrst. (Wednesday after Epiphany, 3 E. 2.)

Extent of Lands, &c., in Westerdale, wapontake of Langbergh. (Sunday after St. Matthew, 1 E. 2.)

Inquisition taken at Southcouton, relative to lands, &c., there, and at various other places; also churches.[1] (Sunday after Ash Wednesday, 1 E. 2.)

Inquisition relative to a rent charge of 10 marks, claimed by the Abbat and Convent of Salley. (Monday after Palm Sunday, 1 E. 2.)

Inquisition concerning lands holden by various persons, as of the Templars, in Schireburn, Bulmer, Rydal, and Thresk. Headed "Foukebring" and "Buckros." (Sunday after St. Matthew, 1 E. 2.) Long.

Inquisition of Templars' lands, &c., in Manor of "Foukebrigg." (Sabbath after Lent, 1 E. 2.)

File of original documents under seal.

No. 1. Geoffrey de Cave's acknowledgment of the receipt of moneys, on account of pension granted to him by the Templars. (London, Wednesday before St. Katharine, 2 E. 2.)

No. 2. Writ to John le Gras, keeper of the Templars' house of Faxflete, directing the said payments. (Westminster, 28th Oct., 2 E. 2.)

No. 3. Indenture testifying payment of pension to Robert de Walton, chaplain, at different times. (2—3 E. 2.)

No. 4. Writ relative to same. (7th May, 1 E. 2.)

No. 5. Recital of Writ (6th May, 1 E. 2) and Inquisition thereon taken, relative to a corrody claimed by Robert de Walton.

Inquisition of Templars' lands at Brampton, within the liberty of Rypon. (Monday after Ash Wednesday, 1 E. 2.)

Patent committing to John le Gras the county and castle of York (*i. e.,* shrievalty); and the lands, goods, and chattels of the Templars, and of Walter de Langton, Bishop of Lichfield and Coventry, late in custody of John de Creppingge. (Westminster, 3rd July, 1 E. 2.) With part of Exchequer Seal attached.

---

[1] Kirkby-fletham and Donnoum (Downholme?) are the churches named as appropriated to the Templars.

No. 1. Original Indenture or Inventory of the store of the Manor of Brampton. (Sunday after St. Margaret, 2 E. 2.)

No. 2. Like of Wilbestayn. (Monday before St. Lawrence, 2 E. 2.)

No. 3. Like (but longer) of Manor of Couton, delivered to Dougal, son of Dual (Mc. Dowel)[1] knight. (29th June 2 E. 2.)

File of Ten Writs and One Inquisition of various dates, 1—2 E. 2, some directing the Sheriff of York, some directing John de Grase, to do various things relative to the Templars and their lands, viz.:

No. 1. To give 4d. a day to each Templar.

No. 2. Certifying a special custody of Manor of Brampton.

Nos. 3, 4. The like of lands in Northdighton, in Manor of Ribstayn.

Nos. 5, 6. The like at Temple Couton.

No. 7. General Writ for the Sheriff to take all the Templars' lands into his custody, in order to a valuation thereof. (Westminster, 25th June, 2 E. 2.)

Nos. 8, 9. To pay a corrody to John de Hopton.

No. 10. To pay a rent charge to the Abbat and Convent of Sallay.

No. 11. Inquisition on same subject.

Inquisition relative to the Templars' Water Mills and certain pieces of land in York, which latter were alleged to belong to the Commonalty of the City of York. (York, Tuesday after Ash Wednesday, 1 E. 2.)

Roll indorsed " Ebor. Prime extente per Vic."

No. 1. Inquisition of lands in Naburn, Coupmanthorp, Staynforde Brigge. (Monday after Ash Wednesday, 1 E. 2.)

No. 2. Extent headed "Foukebring," relative to lands in Pykering, Oketon (Aughton?), Suachthorpe (Sancthorpe?), Galmeton, Willarby, and several other places, written on the margin, the names of which are damaged and obscure. (Sunday after St. Matthias, 1 E. 2.)

No. 3. Inquisitions of lands in the wapontakes of Osgotcrosse and Barkeston. (Potterlowe, Sabbath, 2nd Mar., 1 E. 2.)

No. 4. Fragment of Inquisition relative to Faxflete.

No. 5. Inquisition of lands, &c., in wapontake of Clarhow; viz., the Church of Hunsingovere, lands in North-Dighton, and various other places, the names of which in the margin are

[1] See No. 5 in next File.

damaged and obscure. (Werreby (Wetherby), Sunday after Ash Wednesday, 1 E. 2.)

No. 6. Inquisition of lands, &c., in wapontake of * * * and Morley, imperfect, much damaged, and obscure, covered with goldbeater's skin for preservation on both sides. (Ledes, Sabbath after Ash Wednesday, 1 E. 2.)

No. 7. Original Writ directing John de Gras to deliver the lands, &c., in North Dighton, within the manor of Ribstan, to Philip de Morteyn. (Westminster, 30th April, 1 E. 2.)

No. 8. Recital of same Writ and Extent taken thereon. (Sabbath after St. John ante Port. Lat., 1 E. 2.)

No. 9. Original Writ directing the Sheriff to deliver to Miles de Stapleton the manor of Temple Hirst and the Templars' lands there, also at Birne, Esthirst, Westhathelsay, Middlehathelsay, the manor of Kelyngton with the church there, the grange of Potterlowe, &c. (Westminster, 3rd April, 1 E. 2.)

No. 10. Indenture containing a long inventory of goods at Temple Hirst, some at Potterlawe, and at Welington (Kelington?), the last imperfect. (Wednesday in Easter week, 1 E. 2.)

No. 11. Extent of the manor of Coupmanthorp, and inventory of goods found there. (Monday after invⁿ of the cross, 1 E. 2.)

*** End of the bundle "T. G. 41156."

Separate Roll marked " H. C. H. 3399," being an Indented Roll, with Writ annexed.

No. 1. Original Writ of Privy Seal directing the Sheriff of Yorkshire to deliver to Adam de Hoperton, whom the king had appointed Steward and Keeper of the Manors of Cave, Alwarthorpe, Gritelthorp (Grewelthorpe?), Penhulle, Etton, Wetherby, Brompton, Temple Hurst, Neusom, Whittele, Westendalle, Faxflet, Foukebrigge, Alfanewydale, Hurst, Coupmanthorpe, Ribbeston, lands in Northington (North Otterington?) and Couton, Knapeton, Bainton, and Boutercrombe, with all goods and chattels therein, by indenture between them. (Langele, 15th July, 3 E. 2.)

No. 2. Indenture made accordingly, with great minuteness, and apparently containing the substance of many of the foregoing Records. (Sunday, Feast of St. Laurence, 3 E. 2.)

File of 49 Writs, &c., 5—7 Edw. II., marked "H. C. H. 6826." Many of them are obliterated more or less with age or damp.

* No. 1. Writ relative to allowances out of Hyrst manor.

No. 2. Writ directing wheat and oats, except in manor of Ribbestayn, to be delivered to Sheriff of York.

No. 3. Indenture testifying receipt of such corn.

*No. 4. Writ of allowance to a chaplain.

No. 5. Writ to seize manors of Suth-Cave and Etton, lately committed to David, Earl of Athol, who adheres to Robert de Brus, the king's enemy. (3rd May, 6 E. 2.)

No. 6. Writ to deliver custody of manor of Witherby to Margery, widow of Duncan de Fiendagh.

*No. 7. Indenture containing inventory of goods at Hirst, &c. (Hirst, 1st Dec., 5 E. 2.)

*No. 8. Indenture containing inventory of goods at Coupmanthorp.

*No. 9. Indenture containing inventory of goods at the Mills of York Castle.

No. 10. Writ to allow pension to John de Skelton. (York, 8th Mar., 5 E. 2.)

No. 11. Writ to allow pension to Laurencius de Ebor. (Windsor, 25th Mar., 6 E. 2.)

Nos. 12, 13. Two receipts of the same Laurence.

Nos. 14—17. Like writ for Robert de Bardelby, with three of his receipts.

No. 18. Writ to deliver manor of Faxflete to Joan, widow of Alexander Comyn. (Westminster, 16th Nov., 5 E. 2.)

Nos. 19, 20. Two receipts for Skelton's pension.

Nos. 21, 22. Other Writs, on same affair as No. 18.

Nos. 23, 24. Indentures of delivery of goods at Faxflete.

No. 25. Indenture of delivery of the manor of Penhill and goods there.

Nos. 26, 27. Writs for collecting profits of the churches of * * * and * * * (both damaged).

No. 28. Writ on the same affair as No. 6.

Nos. 29, 30, 31, Writ to allow pension to Robert de Walton; with two of his receipts.

No. 32. Indenture and inventory of delivery of Wetherby; as in Writs Nos. 6, 28.

No. 33. Another Writ on the same subject.

No. 34. Inquisition relative to a carrucate of land, found to belong to the manor of Wetherby. (* * * after feast of St. William of York, A. D. 1312.)

No. 35. Indenture of delivery of manor of Wetherby, by Adam de Hoperton, with inventory (damaged). (5 E. 2.)

No. 36. French letter from David, Earl of Athollc, authorizing the bearer to take to his use the manors of Ettoun and Cave. (St. James, 5 E. 2.)

Nos. 37—39. Writs for delivery of said manors to David, Earl of Athol, &c.

No. 40. Receipt for such delivery, by Andrew le Spenser, bearer of No. 36. (Second week in Lent, 5 E. 2.)

Nos. 41—43. Indentures on such delivery, containing inventories of goods and store. The last is much damaged.

No. 44. Writ for delivery of manor of Neusum.

No. 45. Power of attorney to receive same. (York, 16th Mar., A. D. 1311.)

No. 46—48. Indentures relative to delivery of said manor, with inventories of goods, &c. The first and second are much damaged and hardly legible.

---

* The documents thus marked are those printed in the Gentleman's Magazine, 1857.

Note on p. 16. Jernewic is no doubt Yarnwick near Kirklington, "now depopulated." Walbran's Fountain's Abbey, p. 255.

II.

THE HISTORICAL TRADITIONS OF PONTEFRACT CASTLE, INCLUDING AN INQUIRY INTO THE PLACE AND MANNER OF RICHARD II.'S DEATH.

THE author of the History of Pontefract (Dr. Boothroyd) has given in his title page the following sentence, said to be taken from Swift: "I love Pomfret. Why? 'T is in all our histories; they are full of Pomfret Castle." The present appearance of the place seems scarcely to justify the enthusiasm of the Dean of St. Patrick. The guide to the ruins of the Castle points out the court-yard and other features of the old baronial and regal residence, but the area is occupied by gardens and plantations of liquorice, the produce of which is stored in the dungeons below.

Yet we need only look into our histories to find that they really are full of Pontefract Castle. We know nothing, indeed, of any fortress there in the Roman times, nor more of Pontefract in the Saxon, than that it was probably called Kirkby, though that name does not occur in Domesday, where it is supposed to be included in the manor of Tateshalle, in which Ilbert is said to possess four carucates and sixty *burgenses minutos*, with cotters, villains, and bordars.[1]

The history of the fortress begins with the Conquest and with Ilbert de Lacy.

[1] Facsimile of Yorkshire Domesday, p. xxxviii.

The Norman barons, spoilers living in the midst of those whom they had despoiled, could only hope to retain their lands by the same means by which they had acquired them, and everywhere erected castles of such massive architecture, that they could safely defy the attempts of the ousted and oppressed Saxons to recover what they had lost. Kirkby was pointed out by various circumstances, as a proper site for one of these places of strength. The soil around is very fertile; the hill on which the Castle is built would be nearly unassailable in mediæval warfare, its sides being steep, and its absolute height considerable. Though not upon the Aire,[1] it is sufficiently near to the Roman road which crosses that river at Castleford, to enable its possessors to command this high way to the north and north-west.

Ilbert de Lacy, to whom the lands fell which constituted the Honour of Pontefract, with one hundred and fifty manors in the West Riding,[2] occupied twelve years in building his Castle, which passed for one of the strongest in the kingdom. The De Lacys are conspicuous among the barons of England in the reigns immediately succeeding the Conquest. John de Lacy was one of those appointed, after the signing of Magna Charta, to enforce its execution, Yorkshire and Nottinghamshire being specially assigned to him. He served, too, with great distinction in the Holy Land, and if his epitaph may be believed, was the terror of

---

[1] In Leland's time (Itinerary, 1, p. 40, Hearne's Ed.) a *broken bridge* was seen about half a mile east of Pontefract, which is supposed to have given rise to the name.

[2] Dugdale, Baronage, 1, 98.

all the greatest warriors, Christian and Pagan, of his time.¹ The last of the family, Henry de Lacy, who died in 1312, was one of the most eminent statesmen of the reigns of Edward I. and II.,² and employed by them in various wars and negociations. Having no male heir, his son having been drowned in a well in Denbigh Castle, he had surrendered his lands to the king, who regranted them to him with succession to his daughter, married to Thomas, Earl of Lancaster, who was grandson of Henry III., and cousin to Edward II. In his person the unprecedented number of five earldoms were united, and his wealth and rank of first prince of the blood made him a dangerous antagonist to his feeble sovereign. To strengthen the power of the barons, who aimed at obtaining for their order the control of the administration, Lancaster entered into an unpatriotic alliance with the King of Scots, and came into Yorkshire in the spring of 1322, in the hope of being joined by his Scottish auxiliaries.³ Edward had made a temporary display of vigour, and followed the Earl of Lancaster. A council held at his Castle of Pontefract decided him to march to his own stronghold of Dunstanborough, but his progress to the north was stopped at Boroughbridge, where he was defeated and made

---

[1] Dugdale, 1, 102.—
"Gallus et Hispanus, Normannus Brito quoque Danus,
Almannus gnarus bello, Lumbardus avarus,
Indus et obscenus gentilis, atrox Saracenus,
Ethiopes fusci, Græci, Babylonia, Tusci,
Rex et Soldanus omnis, populus que profanus
Hunc cum cernebant armatum corde tremebant."

He was buried in the Abbey of Stanlaw in Cheshire, afterwards transferred to Whalley.

[2] Dugdale, 1, 104.
[3] Leland, Collect., 1, 461.

prisoner by the sheriff, Sir Simon Ward, and Sir Andrew Harcla, governor of Carlisle. From Boroughbridge he was conveyed by water to York, and thence to Pontefract Castle, which he had recently enlarged and strengthened. A few years before he had witnessed from its towers the ignominious return of the English from the siege of Berwick, and as the king passed, the Earl of Lancaster, with his followers, uttered contemptuous cries against him. Nemesis claimed her right. He was condemned in the presence of the king, without being allowed to plead, and led to execution on a hill over against his castle, mounted on a sorry pony, pelted with mud, and taunted. It was probably from his hostility to Edward and his minions, rather than from his own merits, that his memory was cherished by the common people. Pilgrimages were made to his tomb, and miracles said to have been wrought there, and an unsuccessful application was addressed to the Pope for his canonization.[1] So great was the resort to his tomb, that the government feared it might lead to an insurrection, and fenced it off.[2]

The proceedings against him were reversed in the first parliament of Edward III., and his lands and honours restored to his brother Henry. The Earls of Lancaster, replaced in possession of Pontefract Castle, became again the most powerful of the nobility, and were raised in 1351 to the honour of

---

[1] Lingard, 3, 460.
[2] Rymer, Fœdera, 3, 926. The tomb is said to be at Fryston, in the grounds of Lord Houghton. Archbishop Melton issued an order in 1322, to prevent anyone approaching the tomb for purposes of devotion. Fasti Eboracenses, 405, 6.

the dukedom. John of Ghent, third son of Edward III., married Blanche, the daughter of the first duke, and as she had no brother, and survived her only sister, he reunited the whole of the vast estates of the family, including Pontefract Castle. His second wife, Blanche of Castile, who had fled in terror from the south, during Wat Tyler's insurrection in 1381, sought refuge here; but she was refused admittance by the servants, and was compelled to proceed to Knaresborough.

The wealth and royal descent of this family made it an object of jealousy to the crown, and not without reason; for the son of John of Ghent dethroned Richard, the grandson of Edward III., and under the title of Henry IV. assumed his place. At present I only note the fact, among the events associated with Pontefract Castle, that the deposed sovereign was confined, and according to popular opinion murdered, within its walls. The evidence of this opinion will be the subject of inquiry in a later part of this paper. It became thus again the property of the Crown, and deserving from its strength the name of the key of the north, it was the frequent residence of our kings, when the turbulence of their northern subjects, or the incursions of the Scots, summoned them to this part of their dominions. It was from Pontefract[1] that Henry IV., in revenge for the participation of Archbishop Scrope and the citizens of York in Northumberland's insurrection, issued in 1405 an order to John Stanley and Roger Leeche to take the city into their own hands, with all its liberties

[1] Drake, Eboracum, p. 106, 108.

and privileges. Richard II. had greatly favoured York. He removed the courts of justice hither from Westminster in 1392; sided with the citizens in their disputes with the dean and chapter, and archbishop; gave a sword and mace to be borne before the Lord Mayor, and erected the city into a county. In the civil wars of the next century York always favoured the white rose. The defeat of Northumberland, and Bardolph's rebellion at Bramham in 1408, brought Henry again to Pontefract, and York again felt his displeasure.[1] Many of the prisoners taken in the battle of Agincour in 1415, among them Charles, Duke of Orleans, were sent hither for safe custody. James I. of Scotland, who had been taken prisoner on his way to France, was sent to Pontefract by Henry V. to pass a part of his captivity. Edward IV. spent here the night before the battle of Towton, 1461. Lords Rivers and Gray were confined and executed here, by the orders of Richard III., in 1483. The Tudor sovereigns, Henry VII. and VIII., frequently made Pontefract Castle their residence.

In that reactionary movement against the Reformation, which followed the suppression of the monasteries, and is known as the Pilgrimage of Grace (1536), so well described by Mr. Froude, Robert Aske, its instigator, obtained possession of Pontefract Castle, by the connivance or inactivity of Lord D'Arcy of Temple Hurst; and here, with Lee, Archbishop of York, on the one hand, and Lord D'Arcy on the other, gave audience in the great hall, "with a cruel and inestimable proud

---

[1] Drake, p. 108.

countenance," to the herald of the Earl of Shrewsbury. Within its walls were congregated the representatives of the noblest families of the north, only the Percies, Cliffords, Dacres, and Musgraves having kept aloof. " Such a gathering had not been seen in England, since the grandfathers of these same men fought on Towton Moor."[1] In the same great hall assembled on November 27th in that year, the noblemen and gentlemen whom Aske had called together, to give a sort of parliamentary sanction to his rebellion. From Pontefract Castle went forth the deputation of ten knights, each with ten followers, who carried to the Duke of Norfolk at Doncaster the resolutions of the assembly. They amounted to a re-establishment of the monastic system, which Henry had just destroyed. The restitution of the abbey lands, so earnestly desired by the Commons, could not be agreable to the nobility and gentry who had shared in the spoil. The adherents of the insurrection withdrew or were subdued. Pontefract Castle was occupied by the Duke of Norfolk, and Lord D'Arcy was beheaded on Tower Hill in 1537.

The bloody scenes which had been enacted in the Castle were ominously present to the mind of Wolsey, as, after his fall, he passed Pontefract on his way from Cawood. " Shall I go there," he exclaimed, " and lie there, and die like a beast ?" and he took up his quarters in the Priory.[2] Though it had ceased to be a place of execution, it still

---

[1] Froude, History of England, vol. 3, p. 148. Archæologia, 16, p. 330.

[2] Cavendish, Life of Wolsey, 1, 292. Ed. Singer.

continued to be a state prison, and we find several Scotchmen of rank, who had been taken in the battle of Solway Moss in 1542, committed to Pontefract Castle, under the custody of Sir Henry Savile.[1]

As the state of the country, especially after the union of the crowns, became more settled and tranquil, castles, in the original construction of which strength only had been considered, were altered and improved with a view to comfort; royal fortresses became provincial palaces. In its final enlargement Pontefract Castle comprehended seven acres of ground, and at the commencement of the Civil War, in Charles I.'s reign, it was regarded by the royalists as impregnable. The obstinate resistance which it made to the parliamentary forces corresponded with its character. It was only by three sieges, details of which may be found in the recent volume of the Surtees Society (1860), that it was finally reduced by the parliament in 1649. The second siege had lasted from March 1644 to July 1645. After the third siege the Grand Jury of Yorkshire petitioned the parliament, that the fortifications should be slighted. This was done, and the historical traditions of the Castle were ended. From this time the history of Pontefract is chiefly to be found in parliamentary elections.[2]

With the exception of the Tower of London, no fortress has witnessed such tragic deeds as Pontefract Castle. It is the special object of this

---

[1] Boothroyd's Pontefract, p. 144.
[2] The right of suffrage was the subject of protracted struggle between the burgage tenants and the resiant householders, who finally established their claim.

paper to inquire into the evidence of one of these, the most remarkable of all—the death of Richard II. within its walls. The popular belief has been, that he was assassinated by Sir Piers Exton; historical inquirers have generally rejected this story, but have been divided on the question, whether he died of a broken heart, or perished by voluntary abstinence from food, or by its being withheld from him. Little credence has been given till lately to the rumour, which arose soon after his death, that he had escaped from Pontefract into the Western Isles of Scotland, had been transferred to Stirling, and lived there for nineteen years. Mr. Tytler, however, the able historian of Scotland, has maintained this last opinion in an elaborate argument.[1] The subject has been since discussed by Mr. Amyot in the Archæologia, vols. 23 and 25, by Lord Dover in an address to the Royal Society of Literature, by Sir James Mackintosh[2] and Sir Harris Nicolas, who have all decided against the story of the escape. There is, however, room for a review of the question, and some new evidence has come to light since Mr. Tytler wrote.

It is unnecessary further to recapitulate the history of Richard's fate, than to mention, that having put himself in the power of Henry he was deposed by the sentence of parliament, and conveyed first to Leeds Castle,[3] and ultimately to

---

[1] Historical Remarks on the Death of Richard II., vol. 3, p. 280 (Ed. 1841) of his History of Scotland.

[2] History of England in Lardner's Cyclopædia, p. 381. Lord Macaulay (Hist. 1, 126) adopts the common account of Richard's violent death in Pontefract Castle.

[3] The common histories say, Leeds Castle in Kent, but Whit-

Pontefract, in October 1399. In the first month of 1400, a conspiracy was formed for his liberation, but was defeated at Cirencester, and his brothers, the Earls of Kent and Huntingdon, were put to death. A month later Richard died, or was reported to have died, in his prison. A body, said to be his, was brought to London, and lay in state at the Tower or St. Paul's for several days, the face being uncovered from the forehead to the throat.

Respecting a death which occurred under such circumstances, a variety of rumours were sure to arise. Nothing like a legal inquest took place, and therefore the manner and cause of Richard's death cannot be known with certainty. Creton,[1] who wrote a metrical history of his deposition, maintains that it was Maudelein, Richard's chaplain, and much like him, whose body was brought to London, and that when he wrote, Richard was still living in prison. Walsingham says, he died of voluntary abstinence. The manifesto of the Percies charges Henry with the denial of food to his prisoner. Mr. Tytler says, he died at a good old age in Scotland. The *fact* of his death must be established, before we inquire into the *manner*. The story of

aker has shown that there was in the town of Leeds a castle, dependent on Pontefract. It is supposed to have stood on Mill Hill. Harding's enumeration of the places of his imprisonment is in favour of the Yorkshire Leeds.

"The Kyng then sent King Richard to Ledis
There to be kept surely in privitie.
Fro thens after to Pykering went he nedes,
And to Knavesburgh after led was he;
But to Pauntfrate last, where he did die."
Archæol., 20, p. 205.

[1] Metrical History of the Deposition of King Richard II. Archæol., 20, 221. Creton had been in the service of the deposed king. He wrote in France soon after Richard's death.

the substitution of Maudelein has gained no credit; the only plausible alternative of death at Pontefract is the escape to Scotland.

. The two authorities on which Mr. Tytler chiefly relies are the Scotch historian Bower, the continuator of Fordun, and Wyntoun, author of a rhyming chronicle, who agree in stating that the king was recognized in one of the Western Isles, sent to Donald, then Lord of the Isles, and by him transferred to the Scottish government, by whom he was maintained for many years, till he died in Stirling Castle in 1419. These two authors do not exactly agree; for while Bower says that the fugitive king was serving as a scullion (vilis lixa) in the kitchen of Donald, and was recognized by a fool or jester (fatuus quidam), who had once been attached to Richard's court, Wyntoun represents his discovery as owing to an Irish lady, who had known him in Ireland. Wyntoun, too, says that he denied being the king.

> "Quhen to her mastere she had this tauld
> That man rycht soon he till him cauld,
> And askit him gyf it was swa:
> That he denyit, and said nocht ya."

And concludes his account by saying—

> "Quhethir he had been King or nane
> There was but few that wyst certane."

He seems, indeed, to have been crazy.

> "As he bare him, like was he
> Oft half wod (mad) or wyld to be."

That in spite of his own denial this was the real King Richard is maintained by Mr. Tytler for several reasons. He finds in the Scottish accounts items of charge for the maintenance of "the King of England," and it seems to him incredible that an impostor should have been supported " at great expence," at the Scottish court for eleven years. This expence, however, only amounted in the whole to £733 6s. 8d., or about £66 a year. Never, surely, was a pretender to a crown maintained, for the annoyance of a hostile neighbour,[1] at a cheaper rate. Perkin Warbeck, whom Mr. Tytler admits to have been an impostor, took refuge at the court of James IV., and received from him an annual allowance of £1340, besides extra expences. That the fugitive should be called King of England, entered as such in the accounts, buried as such, and recorded as such upon his tomb, was matter of course. Perkin is always called Duke of York in the Scottish accounts, and had he died in Scotland, instead of being hanged at Tyburn, he would, no doubt, have been styled so in his epitaph.

It is true, that soon after the death of Richard is supposed to have taken place, rumours arose in England that he was still alive. They were of the vaguest kind. At the time of the first conspiracy against Henry, Richard was reported by the conspirators to have escaped from prison, and to be at Pontefract with 100,000 men.[2] Before the battle of Shrewsbury he was said to be at Chester, with a

---

[1] "Whether true or not, it was no unwise policy in Albany, to abstain from giving a public contradiction to the rumour of Richard's being alive, and at times to encourage it, as in this manner he essentially weakened the government of Henry." Tytler, 3, 127.

[2] Tytler, 3, 295, quoting Walsingham and Otterburn.

large force. Whether the existence of such rumours, then or subsequently, deserves the weight which Mr. Tytler attaches to them, may be judged by a few parallel cases, in which deaths of eminent persons, occurring with circumstances of mystery and concealment, have been followed by a persevering popular belief that they had escaped and were alive, political feeling or policy conspiring with the love of the marvellous.

There can be no doubt that Cambyses murdered his brother Smerdis by the hands of Prexaspes;[1] but the manner of "his taking off" was doubtful, and when the Magi plotted to free themselves from the Persian yoke, they represented him to have escaped, and produced a false Smerdis as the true one. Nero had perished in an obscure way,[2] and a false Nero actually made his appearance in the succeeding period, whom the Parthian king maintained at his court, as the regent of Scotland did the supposed Richard.[3] In Russia in the 16th and 17th centuries, after the assassination of the son of John Basilides, no fewer than six pretenders successively appeared, claiming to be the Demetrius who was said to have been murdered. Sigismund, the king of Poland, supported the claim of one of the pretenders. Baldwin, the Latin Emperor of Constantinople, was made prisoner by the Bulgarians, and was either put to

---

[1] Herodotus, 3, 30.
[2] "Nox et ignotum rus fugam Neronis absconderant." Tac. Hist. 3, 68.
[3] Tac. Hist. 1, 2. Sueton. Nero, 57. Zonaras 1, p. 578. Dion Cass. 64, 9. The Christians believed that he would return or revive in the character of Antichrist. Sulp. Sev. 2, p. 367. Aug. de Civ. Dei 20, 19. According to the most probable interpretation, he is the Beast of the Apocalypse, the letters of his name and title, in Hebrew characters, numerically making up 666.

death or died in captivity. Twenty years afterwards there appeared in Flanders a personage, who announced himself to the Flemings as their count, the escaped Emperor, and in spite of the detection of the impostor, the popular voice remained in his favour.[1] Giraldus Cambrensis relates how Harold escaped from the field of Battle, and ended his days in a hermitage, near St. John's Church, Chester. Sebastian of Portugal lost his life at Alcazar, in a battle with the Moors; yet for a century the belief lingered in the national mind that he would appear and claim his throne. In such cases popular credulity is proof against any amount of evidence. The death of the Duke of Monmouth on Tower-hill was a fact as patent and palpable as it could be made. Yet the people of the West fondly believed that he had escaped the axe, by the voluntary sacrifice of one who resembled him, as the English people believed that Maudelein the chaplain of Richard had been substituted for him.[2] The peasantry of Auvergne long refused to believe that Napoleon I. was dead. The Russian Sectaries, who looked upon him as their deliverer, have not yet abandoned the belief that he is living in Turkey and will reappear.[3] Radama II., King of Madagascar, was murdered in 1863; the people believe him to be alive and expect his return.[4]

Mere popular belief therefore, cannot be received as testimony in such cases. Mr. Tytler, however, has graver evidence to produce. Conspiracies, he

---

[1] Gibbon 11, p. 262. 342.
[2] Macaulay, 2, 208. [4] Revue des Deux Mondes,
[3] Stanley, Eastern Church, p. T. 50, p. 998.

says, arose in England in the reign of Henry IV., in which men of rank and fortune hazarded their lives, and these conspiracies were always accompanied with the assertion that Richard was alive.[1] This would have weight, if they had had no motive to profess a belief which they did not honestly entertain; but, true or false, a rumour that Richard was alive was a powerful lever with which to overturn the throne of Henry. Such a belief, however, was not always professed. The manifesto of the Percys in 1403 contained no allusion to Richard's being alive, but charged the king with having starved him to death in Pontefract Castle.[2] It may be said, that the news of his escape had not been brought at this time from Scotland. But in 1405 Northumberland and Archbishop Scrope make no mention of his being alive in Scotland. Their charge against Henry and his accomplices runs thus: "After they had long kept and imprisoned our lord the King, they took him to the Castle of Pomfret, where shortly, as is commonly reported, they harassed and tormented him (vexaverunt et crucifixerunt) for fifteen days and as many nights, in hunger, thirst, and cold, and at last killed him by a death altogether unknown, but by divine grace no longer to be concealed." This death must have been assassination, for the manifesto goes on to say, "Who will feel ashamed to mutilate a common man's son, when these men were not ashamed

---

[1] Hist. of Scotland, 3, 304.
[2] Archæologia, 16, 140. "Thou didst traitorously cause the king, thy lord and ours—a thing horrible to be heard of among Christian people—to be put to death in thy Castle of Pountefract by hunger, neglect (situ al. siti) and cold, during fifteen days."

to mutilate the son of Edward, Prince of Wales?"[1] It is evident that great doubt prevailed as to the manner of Richard's death; of the fact no doubt is expressed. In conclusion the people are exhorted to take up arms on behalf of the Earl of March as their lawful sovereign, which he could not be while Richard lived, being the son of Edward III.'s second son Lionel. In a letter to the Duke of Orleans, soon after Scrope's execution, Northumberland says, indeed, that he had taken up arms "to support the quarrel of King Richard, if alive, and to revenge his death, if he were dead."[2] This may show that some doubt existed, as to whether Richard were not still languishing in prison, as Creton thought when he wrote;[3] but concludes strongly against the story of an escape to Scotland. Of this, if real, Northumberland could not be ignorant, as he was in alliance with Albany, the Regent of Scotland.

The conspiracies which troubled the reigns of Henry IV. and V. arose from mixed motives, among which loyalty to Richard II. was probably the weakest. They were the struggles of a powerful aristocracy, already uneasy under the growing ascendancy of the Crown. In the reigns of weak princes, as Henry III., Edward II., and Richard II., they had been able to make themselves masters of the executive power; under princes of vigour and ability, as Henry IV. and V., they had reason to fear encroachments of royal prerogative. To

---

[1] See the proclamation in the Anglia Sacra, 2, 362.
[2] Lingard, 4, 405, quoting Rot. Parl. 8, 605.
[3] See p. 78.

assume that Richard was alive, and profess to take up arms for his restoration, was a more effective means of annoying the ruling sovereign, than to admit his death, and profess to revenge it, and set the true heir on the throne. After Scrope's defeat in 1405, Northumberland fled into Scotland, and earnestly sought an interview with the supposed fugitive king. But as Bower and Buchanan inform us, he would never grant Northumberland an interview, "fearing," says the latter, "that his imposture should be detected by one who had known his king so well."[1] Northumberland continued to plot against Henry, and lost his life in 1408 in Bardolph's insurrection, but on that occasion it does not appear that he made any profession of belief in Richard's being alive, though rumours of his reappearance were rife in London.[2] We meet with this rumour, but doubtfully and vaguely expressed, in the confession of the Earl of Cambridge, a party to the conspiracy of Gray and Scroop of Masham in 1415. Its object was, if Cambridge's confession has been accurately reported, to proclaim the Earl of March king, provided "yonder man's person which they call King Richard had not been alive, which I wot well he was not alive."[3] The sentence is confused, but it is evident that the rumour of Richard's being alive prevailed, that this belief was to be used to aid the cause of the rebellion, but that Cambridge himself believed Richard to be dead, and his representative an impostor.

Mr. Tytler lays great stress on Lord Cobham's

---

[1] Buchanan, lib. 10, Ann. 1411. [3] Tytler, 3, 320.
[2] Walsingham, p. 376.

declaration, when called upon to plead in 1417, that he declined the authority of the court, since he could acknowledge no judge among them, so long as his liege lord was alive in Scotland. A man about to suffer death for his religious opinions may be justly considered as sincere in his religious profession; but the question was respecting a fact, and it does not appear that Lord Cobham had visited Scotland, and ascertained that his liege lord was alive. Indeed, it was not his part to sift the evidence, on the ground of which he denied the competence of the court before which he was arraigned.

There is another argument which may seem to have some weight. Why, it is asked, did not Henry compel the Scottish Regent to give up the pretended Richard, that he might at once put an end to the rumours of the true king being alive? But had he the power to compel his surrender? He marched into Scotland in 1402, and advanced as far as Leith, but could not even reach Edinburgh, nor does it appear that subsequently he was strong enough to have compelled his surrender, opposed as he would be by all the influence of the French Court, which, though it had no real faith in Richard's being alive, had a strong interest in keeping up a delusion which weakened the power of England, and delayed the misfortunes which befel France in the next reign. Henry had once entertained the project of a truce, if not a perpetual peace with the Scots, on condition that they should transmit to his presence "illum fatuum se dicentem regem Ricardum." He is called in the same document "famulus infatuatus," and "ydolum se dicentem regem Ricardum."[1] Why this negotiation had no result does not appear. By all accounts he was little better than an imbecile. In the year after the battle of Agincourt, the Duke of Orleans, then a prisoner in Pontefract Castle, formed a plot for the march of the Scottish Regent into England, bringing with him the so-called Richard. In the letter in which Henry announces this plot he designates him as the "*mamuel*" or puppet of Scotland, and as such the Scotch and French governments appear to have used him.

These arguments against the story of Richard's escape to Scotland, which had been generally considered decisive by historical inquirers, are thought to have been countervailed by Mr. Williams's work,[2] in which Mr. Tytler's opinion is supported by various arguments. The additional evidence which he has produced is contained in two documents, which have come to light from the Treasury of the Exchequer in the Chapter House, Westminster. Towards the end of the year 1403 an extensive conspiracy against Henry IV. was set on foot, in which the Countess of Oxford, the Abbat of St. John's, Colchester, and others were concerned. Essex and Suffolk appear to have been its principal seat, though Glendower and the Earl of Northumberland were also to have been engaged in it, and a general rendezvous of the confederates was to have taken place at Northampton. Commissioners

---

[1] Amyot, in Archæologia, vol. 23, p. 297.
[2] "Cronique de la Traison et Mort de Richart Deux," edited by Benj. Williams, F.S.A.

were appointed to inquire into the circumstances of the plot, and the examinations of John Prittlewell (or Barrow of Prittlewell in Essex), at whose house the Earl of Huntingdon was seized, after the battle of Cirencester, and Thomas, Abbat of Bileigh, near Maldon, are given by Mr. Williams.[1] The following is the substance of Prittlewell's examination.

A person named William Blyth,[2] in the guise of a knight, sent for him to Bileigh, and told him that he brought him a greeting from his liege lord Richard, who regretted the trouble to which he had been exposed, especially in the matter of the Earl of Huntingdon his brother, and expressed his hope that Prittlewell was the better for Richard's prayers on his behalf. He further offered to swear by the sacrament of two masses which he and Prittlewell had heard together, that three weeks before Christmas (this was Quadragesima Sunday) he parted from King Richard out of a castle in Scotland, the name of which he had forgotten, where he left him alive and in good health. To which Prittlewell replied, that he believed him not, and that he wist well he was not alive, and could not be alive. On which the other said, that he and one Sir John King, who was Sir Harry Percy's priest, and was killed along with Sir Harry [Hotspur] in the battle [of Shrewsbury], went to Pontefract Castle, and spoke with the priest of the Castle, and with a yeoman of Robert of Waterton, who had the charge of King Richard, and that he and the two priests and the yeoman led him out of

---

[1] Appendix to Cronique, p. 269.
[2] He is called also William of Blyth, and was probably a Northumbrian, and agent of the Earl.

the Castle, and set him on horseback, and took him to Northumberland, and so to an isle of the sea, where they kept him till they had made a treaty with Scotland, and the council had determined that the Lord Montgomery should have charge of him. He further offered to swear, that he had three letters from Richard, between Christmas and Quadragesima Sunday, when this interview took place, and three tokens to Queen Isabella, with which he had been three times to her in France. The queen, he said, had been long at sea, and had suffered so much from it that she had landed with all her horse at Esclus; and he offered to swear that he would bring him to Queen Isabella or King Richard within fifteen days. Prittlewell concludes his deposition in these words: "My unready wit would not have served me, but that I should have believed much of his matters, had it not been that by the grace of God, *I found him out in two false lies*. First, that he said he was brought up in King Richard's household from a child, and I well knew the contrary; the other, that he said he was at the battle with Sir Harry Percy, and there Sir Harry Percy made him knight, and no more than him; and he said that Sir Harry and he were both armed in Sir Harry's coat armour, which I wist well was false, by true men that were at the battle, that saw Sir Harry both quick and dead."

The evident object of these falsehoods was to gain credit for himself, as intimately acquainted with King Richard, and in confidential relations with the Northumberland family. What security have we that his account of his conducting Richard from Pontefract to Scotland was not a third lie, framed for a similar purpose?

Another deposition or confession is that of the Abbat of Bileigh, to whom the same person, William Blyth, came on the same errand. To him he represented himself as sent by the Earl of Northumberland, who had given him a great gilded girdle, and had advised him to go as a knight. According to his statement to the Abbat, he had a sealed patent from King Richard, to be published as soon as it should be known which way the people inclined; that Richard was coming out of Scotland, and Queen Isabel and the Duke of Orleans from France, and Glendower from Wales; and all were to meet at Northampton. The Abbat of Colchester, who was implicated in the same plot, had said to the Abbat of Bileigh, that he had sent a man with a ring to Scotland, and told him, if Richard were alive he should come again with the ring. He accordingly returned, and brought word that Richard was alive. Whether he had previously known the king, whether he saw him, what evidence of the fact he brought back, does not appear. A Richard was indeed forthcoming, not the King of England, however, but Thomas Warde of Trumpington,[1] who personated him.

Now if we believe Blyth's account to Prittlewell, Richard was in regular correspondence with himself and his queen, as well as with the malcontents in England. None of these parties, therefore, could have the smallest doubt that he was alive. Let us see how their words and actions accord with the

[1] Lingard, 4, 398.

supposition of their possessing such knowledge. Hotspur's priest was the companion of Blyth in the enterprise of delivering Richard from prison, and conducting him to the Western Isles. The escape must have taken place early in A. D. 1400; the insurrection of the Percys was in the middle of 1403. The priest was at Shrewsbury, and lost his life in the battle. Is it credible, that Hotspur and his father, knowing Richard to have escaped and to be alive in Scotland, instead of calling on the people of England to rally round the standard of their lawful sovereign, should have justified their rebellion by alleging (see p. 83) that Henry had murdered him by cold and hunger in Pontefract Castle? And again, in Northumberland and Scrope's rebellion in 1405, the design avowed is not to set Richard on the throne again, but to avenge his death.

If Blyth's tale be true, the French Court and Queen Isabella must have had abundant proof that Richard was alive; he had carried tokens[1] to her from her husband, and had letters and documents from his hand. Yet the Count de St. Pol, the brother-in-law of Richard, in 1402 sent a herald to Henry, with a message of defiance, in which he

---

[1] There could be no difficulty in sending tokens from a supposed Richard, since his former chamberlain Serle, according to his own confession, had used various means to persuade people that the king was alive in Scotland, though he did not himself believe it. The Countess of Oxford had little figures of stags made in silver and gold to be distributed as tokens from the captive king, while the Essex insurrection was hatching. The leaning of the king and his father, the Duke of Lancaster, towards the principles of Wickliffe may have disposed these two Abbats and other ecclesiastics to join in an insurrection against him.

says he is notoriously accused of the death of Richard, and declares that "God knows how it happened." He should incur the indignation of God and men if he did not do all in his power to revenge his death.[1] This was two years subsequent to the time of Richard's alleged escape from Pontefract. The challenge of the Duke of Orleans, in the same year, is equally distinct in its allegation of murder against Henry. Now if Richard had escaped in disguise and alone from Pontefract, and been accidentally discovered, as the Scotch say, as a scullion in the Western Islands, we could understand that the rumour of his death had been superseded, after a considerable interval, by evidence of his being alive in Scotland. But it was not so. He had been conveyed from Pontefract, according to Blyth, by a cavalcade of four persons, who deposited him in Scotland, and who therefore could furnish such proof of his escape as would have precluded all doubt.

Much stress has been laid upon the circumstance, that Isabella was about to land in England in 1403, as a proof that she believed him to be living. Of this the only evidence is the testimony of William Blyth, and it may have been another of his "false leasings." It is not in itself at all incredible, that a French descent was meditated in conjunction with the English rising. But there was a sufficient motive, in the relations between England, France, and Scotland, for co-operation between the two latter powers for the overthrow of Henry, without a belief on the part of either that

[1] Monstrelet, vol. 1, p. 55. Johnes' Ed.

Richard was really alive. The councils of France were already distracted by the jealousy of the Dukes of Burgundy and Orleans. The Duke of Burgundy was desirous of amity with England, for the sake of his subjects in Flanders, to whom commerce with England was essential; the Duke of Orleans was bent on war; it was of his own motion, and without the knowledge of the Council of State, that he had sent his defiance to Henry, and equally without their consent, he had instigated the Count de St. Pol to follow up his challenge, by an attack upon the English fleet, and a descent on the islands of the Channel.[1] After the death of the Duke of Burgundy he entered into an alliance with Owen Glendower, whom he promised to assist with a fleet and an armed force, and endeavoured to engage the Spaniards to make an attempt on Calais. To ally themselves with France for the annoyance of England was the steady policy of the Scottish sovereigns and statesmen, and at this time they were naturally eager to revenge themselves upon Henry for the defeat which they had suffered the year before at Homildon Hill. If Isabella really accompanied an expedition intended to aid in the English insurrection, it must have been as a measure of state policy, which would be much aided by her apparent belief that Richard was still alive.[2]

The detail of Richard's escape from Pontefract in Blyth's narrative may be thought to give it credibility, but if examined it has a contrary effect.

[1] Sismondi, Hist. des Français, 8, 159.   [2] Archæologia, 20, 427.

The Scotch historians, the original authorities for his escape, say that he was discovered in the kitchen of the Lord of the Isles, acting as a scullion. But if Blyth's account be true, he had been escorted from Pontefract to the Isles by those who had effected his escape, so that no doubt could be entertained who he was, or whence he came. The passage of such a company through such an extent of country without detection is less credible than the previous supposition, that he had wandered alone and in misery to the Isles, and had there taken menial service with Donald their lord. The disappearance of the prisoner, along with a yeoman of the Castle who had the charge of him, must have been known at the latest in a few hours; a single person might have lurked in the woods, or found shelter in cottages, but a company of five persons, one on horseback, could be tracked without difficulty. The escape therefore may be pronounced impossible, without the complicity of Sir Robert Waterton. Whatever *law* we may suppose the fugitives to have had, the news of the escape must have been known soon enough for pursuit to have been made, of which there is no trace. Was Henry likely, when he heard his rival had vanished, to satisfy himself with the notion that it would be an easy matter to feign a death in Pontefract Castle, to carry a false Richard in funeral procession to London, to expose him there, and afterwards to inter him? Surely we should have heard of active measures, if not to arrest the fugitives, at least to take vengeance on those who had allowed or abetted the escape. Of this vengeance Waterton would be the first object. Yet so far was he from incurring Henry's displeasure, that he retained him in his service, and sent him after the battle of Shrewsbury to encounter the Earl of Northumberland. Would so politic a sovereign have treated in this way one who had grossly neglected, if he had not violated, his trust?

We are brought back, then, to Pontefract Castle as the place of Richard's death; but how was it effected? The manifesto of Scrope seems to point to some brutal violence, succeeding a period of prolonged torture by privation of food. Fabyan, Hall, and Holinshed give a definite form to the story of assassination, and assign Sir Piers Exton as the executioner. Wolsey's exclamation, before referred to, (p. 75) evidently alludes to death by the blow of a poleaxe, and Shakespeare fixed it for ever in the popular mind. With the instinct of dramatic genius he perceived how much more impressive such a catastrophe would be, than death by thirst and hunger. The pictures of Richard's resignation and patience, as he rides into London beside Bolingbroke, or moralizes in his dungeon at Pontefract, are eminently beautiful; but we are glad to find that the fire of valour still lurks in the son of the Black Prince, under the ashes of repentance and humiliation, and blazes out at last in an act of vigorous self-defence. We feel that he has died as a King should die. The pen of Dante, or the pencil of Reynolds, may give a powerful interest to death by famine, but what avails for poetry or painting may be wholly unsuited to dramatic action. Besides, Richard's was a solitary prison, and what would Ugolino's Tower of Famine have been, without the presence of his sons, whose fate wrings their father's heart, far more than his own bodily suffering? Gray, on the other hand, wishing to contrast the splendour and promise of Richard's opening life with his miserable death, adopts the story of his perishing by thirst and hunger.

> "Close by the regal chair,
> Fell Thirst and Famine scowl
> A baleful smile upon their baffled guest."

Shakespeare recurs to the death of Richard in the second part of Henry IV., where, speaking of Archbishop Scrope, he says,—

> "He's followed both with body and with mind,
> And doth enlarge his rising with the blood
> Of fair King Richard, scraped from Pomfret stones."

He probably speaks metaphorically, and only means that Scrope used the supposed murder of Richard, as a topic to inflame the resentment of the people. At all events, a literal exhibition of the blood would not be regarded by the historical critic as a proof of his having died by violence. Every one who has visited the scenes of memorable transactions must have observed, how readily material evidences are supplied in support of the traditions of the place.[1] The post round which Richard fled to escape his murderers, still marked with "cruel hackings and fierce blows," was shown to visitors

---

[1] It is an ancient practice. When Pausanias, the geographer, visited Sparta, he was shown, hanging from the roof of a temple, the egg from which Castor and Pollux had been hatched. 3, 16, 2. Still more extraordinary was the exhibition at Lavinium of the sow, "triginta capitum fetus enixa" (Æneid, 3, 391) kept in pickle. "Corpus matris ab sacerdotibus, quod in salsura fuerit, demonstratur." Varro, R. R., 2, 4, 18.

in the 17th century.[1] The inspection of Richard's tomb in Westminster Abbey so far discredited the common story, that it showed the skull to be entire, with the exception of a small cleft, produced by the opening of one of the sutures.[2]

If Richard neither escaped to Scotland, nor was assassinated by Sir Piers Exton, there remains only death by hunger to be considered. And this question again subdivides itself into two,—death by voluntary abstinence from food, or by its being withheld from him by his keepers, Swinburn and Waterton. The former mode rests upon the authority of Walsingham before quoted. He says, that on hearing of the disastrous issue of the attempt made by the Earls of Kent and Salisbury, in the beginning of 1400, to restore him, he determined to end his life by voluntary abstinence from food, and died on St. Valentine's day.[3] Thomas of Otterburn, also a contemporary, says, that he had determined to starve himself to death, but repented, and wished to take food; "the orifice of the stomach, however, having been closed," he was unable to do it, and consequently sunk.[4] Whether the phrase is medically correct or not, it is quite

---

[1] Archæol., 23, p. 281; note C, p. 311.

[2] King in Archæol., 6, 313. Gough's Sepulchral Monuments, vol. 1, pt. 2, p. 165, 166, where may be seen the leonine inscription on his tomb,—

 Prudens et mundus | Ricardus jure secundus
 Per fatum victus | jacet hic sub marmore pictus
 Verax sermone | fuit et plenus ratione, &c.

[3] Walsingham's words are, "inedia voluntaria ut fertur." In a MS. poem on King Edward IV. in the Collection of the Society of Antiquaries, it is said of Henry of Derby, "He toke this rightwys kyng, Goddes trew knight, And hym in prison put perpetuelly, Pyned to deth, alas! ful pyteuxly." Journ. of Arch. Assoc., 6, p. 128.

[4] Tytler, 3, 292.

conceivable that by long abstinence the stomach might be so much weakened, as to render the attempt to take food unavailing. The vacillating character of Richard renders it not improbable, that he might abandon the purpose which he had formed of starving himself to death. Scrope's proclamation and the manifesto of the Percys distinctly charge Henry with keeping his prisoner from food and drink. Harding's expression, that he was "forehungered," is ambiguous, but points to enforced, rather than voluntary starving.

That Richard was really in a languishing state of health, immediately after his consignment to Pontefract Castle, appears from the minutes of the Council in February 1400.[1] The first runs thus: "If Richard, the late king be living, as is supposed, let him be well and securely kept, for the safety of the king and his kingdom." The second is: "It seems expedient to speak to the king, that in case Richard the late king be still living, he be placed in security, according to the desire of the peers of the kingdom; and if he have departed this life by any kind of death, that he should be shewn openly to the people, in order that they may have knowledge of it." It should seem from the second minute that the council did not know where Richard was, as they could hardly desire a place of greater security for him than Pontefract Castle. It is singular that in both they should speak doubtfully on such a point as whether Richard was living or not. But intelligence did not reach London from Pontefract in those days so rapidly

[1] Archæologia, 25, 391.

as in ours, and the treatment of the dethroned king was probably one of those *arcana* of state, which Henry kept in his own breast.

We have only presumptions and probabilities, therefore, to guide us, in deciding on Henry's guilt or innocence in the matter of Richard's death. If, on the one side, it may be urged, that the execution of his friends and relatives taken at Cirencester was likely to make him weary of life; on the other it may be said, that as the object of the conspiracy was to set him at liberty and on the throne, Henry had a powerful motive for immediately putting him to death. He certainly took no means to establish the fact of Richard's voluntary death. He replied to the charge of the Percys by an army, to the challenge of the Duke of Orleans by an offer of single combat. Henry's personal character would incline me to the belief, that he was not accessary to his predecessor and cousin's death. Our history is black with unquestionable crimes, and we would wish to believe, that Pontefract does not share with Berkley and Corfe Castles the bad eminence of having witnessed the murder of a king. Considering Henry as arraigned before the tribunal of History, a Scottish judge would, I think, on the evidence produced, direct the jury to find a verdict of "Libel not proven;" an English judge would advise them to give the culprit the benefit of their doubts; while both would concur in treating the Scotch *alibi* as a fiction.

III.

THE RELATION OF COINS TO HISTORY, ILLUSTRATED FROM ROMAN COINS DISCOVERED AT METHAL NEAR WARTER, AND PRESENTED TO THE YORKSHIRE PHILOSOPHICAL SOCIETY BY THE RIGHT HONBLE. THE LORD LONDESBOROUGH AND W. RUDSTON READ, ESQ.[1]

It seems due to the donors of the coins to which this paper refers, that they should not be consigned to our cabinets, without an attempt being made to render them subservient to the instruction of our members. It is true that a numismatist would not consider them as of great value; there is hardly any one among them to which he would affix his R. They are of minute size, of coarse workmanship, of debased metal, and ordinary types. These circumstances, which make the collector view them with indifference, do not prevent their having a great historical interest. The smallness of their intrinsic value, and the rudeness of their execution, is a reflexion of the empoverished times in which they were produced, and the low condition of art. All such objects of antiquity tend to give definiteness and certainty to our historical conceptions. When we merely read history, its characters pass

---

[1] See Report of Yorkshire Philosophical Society for 1856. The Roman road from Market Weighton to Millington, probably the Delgovitia of Antonine's Itinerary, must have passed near the place of their discovery. See Newton's Map of Roman Yorkshire.

before us, very much like the shadows of a phantasmagoria; but when we see the armour in which the men of fifteen centuries ago fought, the household vessels in which they prepared or took their food, and the coins which passed through their hands, we feel that they were realities, and of kin to ourselves.

The series of coins presented by Lord Londesborough to the Society, begins with Valerian, includes Gallienus and the period of the so-called Thirty Tyrants, and ends with Aurelian, comprehending seventeen years, 253—270. It may be convenient to exhibit its events in a chronological table.

A. D.
253. P. Licinius VALERIANUS, who commanded the Gallic and German legions, is chosen Emperor. He associates his son, Publius Licinius Gallienus, with himself.
257. The Goths invade the provinces south of the Danube, and Sapor the eastern provinces.
258. Postumus elected Emperor by the Gauls.
260. Valerian defeated and made prisoner near Edessa.
261. GALLIENUS sole Emperor.
265. Postumus killed by his soldiers.
268. Death of Gallienus and accession of CLAUDIUS GOTHICUS.
270. Death of Claudius and temporary dominion of QUINTILLUS. Accession of AURELIAN.
275. Death of Aurelian and accession of TACITUS.
276. Death of Tacitus and accession of PROBUS.

The history of this period has a sort of epic unity. The reign of Valerian, with which it opens, exhibits the deepest degradation which the majesty of the Roman Empire ever underwent. The aged emperor was taken prisoner by the Persian king, Sapor, who made use of his neck as a footstool from which to mount his horse,[1] and after his death caused his skin to be stuffed with hay and exhibited in one of the temples.[2] During the reign of Gallienus, the dismemberment of the empire seemed imminent; its frontiers suffered from the invasion of the barbarians, and its interior provinces from insurrection and civil war. Claudius Gothicus, the successor of Gallienus, repelled the Alemanni from Italy, and drove the Goths from Greece. Aurelian restored the unity of the empire, by putting an end to the power of Tetricus in the west and Zenobia in the east, suppressed the factions of Rome, and surrounded the city with a wall of such circuit and strength, that she seemed secure from the attacks of the barbarians. Coins of Tacitus and Probus, not included in Lord Londesborough's donation, were found in the same hoard, and as the latest marks the earliest date at which the deposit can have been made, we may probably assign it to some time in the reign of Probus, who was assassinated by his soldiers in 282 at Belgrade.

Only three coins of VALERIAN are found in the present collection, of which two are partially illegible. His reign was supposed to be going on, while he was a captive in Persia, and coins were struck, and laws promulgated in his name by his son Gallienus, as still being emperor. The chronology of his coinage is therefore hopelessly obscure. He had passed through a long gradation of honours, had been selected by an unanimous vote of the Senate as the worthiest man to fill the high office of Censor, and

---

[1] Aurel. Victor.   [2] Agathias, 4, 23.

when Gallus had been put to death by his soldiers, and the usurper Æmilianus had shared the same fate, Valerian was chosen as the successor of Gallus. He was at the head of the legions of Gaul and Germany, but he appears, a rare distinction in this age, to have owed the throne to his merits, and not to the purchased votes either of the soldiery or the populace. But of his reign we know little, except his defeat and captivity; the Augustan historian declining to dwell upon his history, as being familiar to those for whom he wrote, and through regret for a fate so unworthy of his virtues. "Pudet altius virum extollere, qui fatali quadam necessitate superatus est."[1] Valerian has been blamed by Gibbon,[2] for associating with himself in the empire his son Gallienus, instead of one of many able generals, who were better qualified to defend it. It is natural to attribute this to the weakness of paternal affection; but, on the other hand, if Valerian, when he proceeded to the east to attack the Persians, had left a stranger in blood on the throne of the west, the disruption of the empire would have been the certain consequence. Gallienus maintained his allegiance during the captivity of his father, and appears not to have assumed the honours of sole emperor till after his death.

The misfortunes of the Roman Empire from the captivity of Valerian to the reign of Claudius Gothicus, have been generally attributed to the weakness and vices of his son, GALLIENUS. The history of this emperor has been derived from two

[1] Trebellius Pollio, Valerianus, c. 3. [2] Ch. 10, vol. 1, p. 411.

sources, neither of which has escaped the imputation of partiality. The Augustan historian Trebellius Pollio, who is by far the fullest in detail, and who gives a most unfavourable view of his character, dedicates his biography to Constantine, who traced his own descent from Claudius Gothicus, whom the soldiers substituted for the son of Gallienus, after the father had been assassinated in the camp before Milan. On the other hand, Zosimus,[1] who makes no mention of the frivolous and cruel acts which Trebellius attributes to Gallienus, but describes him as an active and vigorous ruler, being himself a pagan, was hostile to Constantine, by whom Christianity was established.[2] The character which Gallienus usually bears in history is summed up in the epigrammatic words of Gibbon: "In every art that he attempted, his lively genius enabled him to succeed; and as his genius was destitute of judgment, he attempted every art, except the important ones of war and government. He was a master of several curious but useless sciences, a ready orator, an elegant poet, a skilful gardener, an excellent cook,—and a most contemptible prince."[3] We have seen strange reversals of the judgments of history on character, or at least strenuous appeals with the view of obtaining a reversal. Mr. Mitford has whitewashed Dionysius the Tyrant; Mr. Grote has exalted Cleon to the rank of a patriot; Mr. Froude has recoined Henry VIII. into a champion of the civil and religious liberties of England. I am not going to undertake a similar office for

[1] Lib. 1, c. 30—40.
[2] Lib. 2, c. 29.
[3] Decline and Fall, ch. 10, vol. 1, p. 412.

Gallienus, or to justify the encomiastic language of his arch at Rome : " GALLIENO CLEMENTISSIMO PRINCIPI CUJUS INVICTA VIRTUS SOLA PIETATE SUPERATA EST;" but I think a careful reader of his life in the Augustan History must be struck by the writer's desire to give an unfavourable turn to all his words and actions, if they were in any way doubtful. He admits that he performed many valiant deeds, but says they were outnumbered by disgraceful actions. His valour he calls sudden daring.[1] He says it was on account of his indolent character that the army did not make him emperor after the captivity of his father, though he was already associated with Valerian in the empire, and therefore no such election was necessary.

Gallienus seems to have suffered, as others have done, for his quickness in repartee and his propensity to give serious things a ludicrous turn. When told that Egypt had revolted, he replied, " Can't we do without Egyptian linen ? " When Asia was ravaged by the Goths, and was suffering also from earthquakes, he said, " Can't we do without their flower of nitre ? " And when Gaul was lost, he smiled and asked, " Shall we be ruined if we get no Atrebatian plaids ? " There may, however, have been policy in thus treating lightly the losses of the empire when others were disheartened by them; and the true way of judging, whether his laughter was the laughter of a fool or not, is to enquire, whether all ended with a joke. Now in all these cases we find, that Gallienus took measures to repair the losses. His general Theodotus made

[1] Erat in Gallieno subita virtutis audacia. Treb. Pollio, c. 8.

prisoner Æmilianus, who had raised Egypt in revolt, and sent him in chains to Gallienus. The same Theodotus led an army against Postumus, who had revolted in Gaul, and Gallienus himself, according to Trebellius, "longo bello tracto per diversas obsidiones ac prælia, rem modo feliciter modo infeliciter gessit." This looks like something more than a "subita virtutis audacia," which is all that Trebellius allows him. The Goths were driven out of Asia by his generals, and if he took a cruel vengeance on Byzantium, we must remember what were the usages of war in those days. The Goths were ravaging Illyricum; Gallienus marched against them, surprized them, and slew great numbers. This Trebellius calls an accident. A more candid historian would perhaps have said, that it was owing to the rapidity of his movements, and the prudence with which he concealed them.[1] In short, I think, however contemptible Gallienus may have been for his vices, he was not a contemptible sovereign. No doubt he was not the man that the age required; he probably felt it, and, had he known Shakespeare, he might have said with Hamlet:

> "The time is out of joint; O cursed spite
> That ever I was born to put it right!"

His death was that of a soldier. While he was engaged in war with the Goths, Aureolus, with the

---

[1] Gallienus ut erat nequam et perditus ita etiam, ubi necessitas coegisset, velox, fortis, vehemens, crudelis. Treb. Pollio, Hist. Aug. 2, 270. Julian was subjected to the same depreciatory comments. He was called, "loquacem talpam, litterionem Græcum, segnem et timidum et umbratilem." Amm. Marc., 17, 11. Gibbon judges him more favourably than he does Gallienus.

Illyrian legions, revolted and entered Italy. Gallienus marched to Milan against him. A false alarm was given at night in the camp, planned, according to Zosimus (1, 41), by Heraclianus, that Aureolus was approaching to attack with his army. Gallienus rose hastily from supper, and putting on his armour, and giving the word to his troops to follow, rode, without waiting for his body guards, to meet the supposed enemy; and was killed by a præfect of the Dalmatian Cavalry. Trebellius,[1] though so unfavourable to him, acknowledges that the soldiers broke out into sedition, and complained that they had been robbed of a commander; "utilem, necessarium, fortem, efficacem;" and it was only by a bribe of twenty aurei a piece, paid out of the treasures of Gallienus, that they were induced to decree that "Tyrant" should be subjoined to his name in the Fasti.[2]

The rise of the Thirty Tyrants is usually connected with his reign, and attributed to his weakness, though some of them, as Æmilianus, Ingenuus, and Postumus, had started up before the captivity of Valerian. It is well understood that the word *Tyrant*, as applied to them, means nothing more than an assumption of imperial power, without the authority of the Senate. Thus on the tomb of the two Victorini at Cologne was inscribed, "Hic duo Victorini Tyranni siti sunt."[3] The number of thirty was chosen by the Augustan historian, because a celebrated tyranny at Athens had consisted of that number, and to complete it,

---

[1] Hist. Aug., 2, 267.
[2] Hist. Aug., 2, 230.
[3] Hist. Aug., 2, 267.

he acknowledges that he had included a name or two about which he was uncertain whether the owner had exercised imperial power, and also females, as Victorina and Zenobia, "tyrannesses," "tyrannas aut tyrannidas."[1] He himself eulogizes several of them, as men of high merit and military skill. The real number appears to have been nineteen.

Sir Francis Palgrave, in his Rise and Progress of the English Commonwealth (ch. 11), has given a view of the so-called Tyrants, which is well deserving of attention. He considers them as in no sense usurpers of dominion, but as patriotic men, who seeing that the Empire was in a state of dissolution, and that the central authority was unable to provide for the defence of the provinces, set up independent governments, with the assent of the armies and the people of those provinces, and so preserved them from the invasion of the Barbarians. They were, in short, according to Sir Francis, the forerunners of the founders of the kingdoms of the west. It is certain that in this age, when the real power of election lay in the armies, and the Senate only ratified the choice of the strongest, it is difficult to draw the line between legitimacy and usurpation. And seeing the controversy which still goes on, about the merits of Cæsar, and Cromwell, and the two Napoleons, it would be a hopeless task to analyse the motives of Victorinus, Postumus, and Tetricus, and assign their several proportions to ambition and patriotism. But I think we cannot be wrong

---

[1] Hist. Aug., 2, 231.

in rejoicing that their attempts failed. Had the Roman Empire been dismembered at this period, the probability is, that paganism would have continued predominant in the separated portions; for the power of Constantine, when sole emperor, was barely adequate to the establishment of Christianity. But however this might have been, if they had repelled the Barbarians, which Trebellius (2, 259) says was the effect of the assumption of power by Postumus, and the kingdoms which they formed had become permanent, they would have perpetuated the vices of the Roman Empire. Like slips taken from a blighted and decaying tree, they would have had no healthy vitality. This new life was to be infused by the settlement of the Teutonic nations. What Europe might have been, had the formation of its separate kingdoms preceded that infusion, we may judge from the history of the Byzantine Empire. It escaped for several centuries barbarian conquest, but it only languished on, in a state of decrepitude, while in western Europe a new æra of knowledge and liberty was inaugurated, which proceeded in a course of steady, though slow, development.

If any portion of the Western Empire could have preserved itself in the age of Gallienus, as an independent monarchy, it would seem to be Gaul; and if any of the Thirty Tyrants fully corresponded with Sir F. Palgrave's description, it would be Postumus, as he is described by Trebellius.[1]

---

[1] Vir in bello fortissimus, in pace constantissimus, in omni vita gravis, c. 8. Yet with these qualities "more illo quo Galli novarum rerum semper sunt cupidi, Lolliano agente interemptus est." Ibid. In this respect how little has the nation changed!

According to him, he was chosen by the army and the people of Gaul, who had decreed the death of Saloninus, the son of Gallienus, and, during a government of seven years, restored the prosperity of the Gallic nation, and earned their gratitude, by driving out their German invaders. Trebellius, however, confesses that the majority of authors alleged, that Gallienus having entrusted his son to the care of Postumus, Postumus put him to death, and assumed the imperial authority; Zosimus distinctly asserts this; nor has Trebellius any evidence to countervail the current belief, except that "ejus non conveniat moribus," it is inconsistent with his character, that he should have committed such a crime. I fear that history, and especially the history of this age, will hardly allow us to push the argument from character so far. But it appears to be quite true, that under Postumus and his successor Tetricus, (the reigns of Lollianus, Victorinus, and Marius in Gaul having been short may be passed over,) Gaul enjoyed a period of internal peace and prosperity, and that its frontiers were not only defended from the invasion of the German nations, but military stations established beyond the Rhine. In this age Britain (as, indeed, Spain) usually followed the fortunes of Gaul, either under a legitimate division of the empire, or in cases of usurpation. Of the 150,000 troops, whom Albinus, after assuming the purple in Britain, led to encounter Severus at Lyons,[1] a large part must have been Gauls and Spaniards; and after his defeat, Severus put to death great numbers of the

---

[1] Comp. Dion. Cass., 75, 5.

chief men of these two countries, as his partizans. Bonosus and Proculus, who assumed the imperial authority at Cologne, claimed to themselves not Gaul only, but Spain and the Britannic Isles;[1] and when Diocletian associated three Cæsars with himself, Gaul, Spain, and Britain were allotted to Constantine. Indeed, it was impossible that Britain should long be held by a power seated in Rome, if Gaul, which included all the harbours of the Channel, was in hostile hands. We need not be surprised, therefore, that the coins of Postumus, Victorinus, and Tetricus, though Gaul was the chief seat of their authority, should be abundant in Britain, and especially in York and Aldborough, since York was the capital of Britain. Lord Londesborough's donation alone contains 192 of Victorinus and 585 of Tetricus the elder. The great abundance of the coins of Carausius and of Constantine and his family, in York and the neighbourhood, may be explained by the same cause.

When Horsley wrote, no inscribed monument of any of the Thirty Tyrants had been discovered in Britain; but since then, three have been dug up at Clausentum (Bittern near Southampton) dedicated to Tetricus;[2] one to Postumus near Brecknock;[3] and to Piavonius Victorinus at Pyle near Swansea.[4]

At Durobrivæ (Caistor near Peterborough) an inscription has been found to Florianus, the half-brother of the Emperor Tacitus, who had proposed him for consul only a short time before his own

---

[1] Hist. Aug., 2, 671.
[2] Winchester Congress of Arch. Assoc., p. 163.
[3] Archæol., 4, p. 7. Orelli, 1015.
[4] Journal of Arch. Assoc., 2, 298.

assassination. Florianus, who assumed the empire on his brother's death, opened his own veins two months after at Tarsus, on hearing that the legions of Syria were in arms against him.

No time seems to have been lost in conferring on a new emperor the marks of sovereignty. Lord Londesborough's donation contains coins of Marius, who is said to have reigned only three days. His history is a striking example of the way in which during this period men were raised to the imperial dignity, and of the peril which accompanied it. After Victorinus, Lollianus, and Postumus had been put to death, he was made Imperator. He had been a *faber ferrarius*, commonly translated a blacksmith, but his trade appears to have been that of a sword-cutler, though his uncommon muscular strength, which enabled him to stop a waggon in motion with his forefinger, and break a man's head with a blow of two fingers, savours of the smithy. His fate was characteristic. He had insulted a soldier, formerly a workman of his, who, when he stabbed him, told him the sword came from his own manufactory. Nineteen different types appear upon his coins, which are so numerous, considering his short reign, as to have much perplexed numismatists. It is conjectured that he had been already proclaimed emperor in the western part of Gaul, and that the legions on the Rhine recognized his authority. The three days of which Trebellius speaks, would then be the interval between this recognition and his assassination.[1]
QUINTILLUS, the brother of Claudius Gothicus is

[1] Cohen, Médailles Impériales, 5, 76.

said to have reigned only seventeen days; we have nine of his coins. They are by no means rare, and they exhibit more than fifty different types. Zosimus [1] makes his reign to have lasted several months.

Of all the Tyrants, Tetricus was the only one who did not come to a violent end. CLAUDIUS GOTHICUS during his reign of two years did not molest him, but Aurelian having reconquered the east, marched into Gaul against Tetricus, who still held that province, along with Spain and Britain. The armies met in the plains of Chalons-sur-Marne, and the troops of Tetricus were defeated. Tetricus himself, though he had probably been in secret understanding with Aurelian, was carried in triumph with his son, but was afterwards invested by Aurelian with high office. The heads of Aurelian and Tetricus are even found united on the same coin.[2] By the victories of Aurelian the unity of the Roman Empire was for a time restored.

It is impossible not to be struck with the irregularity of form, the low value, and the general meanness of execution, which characterize this collection. Their irregular outline probably arose from the want of machinery for cutting the disks of an uniform size. From the confusion which prevailed before and after the reign of Valerian, a debasement of the coinage was naturally to be expected. The silver coin of this period is exceedingly base, and some of what at first sight appears so is brass, washed with silver or tin. It is not

---

[1] I, 47.   [2] Num. Journal, 14, 49.

till the reign of Diocletian that good silver reappears.[1]

One of the first undertakings of Aurelian was to punish those who had been concerned in the debasement, especially of the gold coinage.[2] He gives an extraordinary account of this transaction, in a letter to the Consul Ulpius, preserved by the historian Vopiscus.[3] Being headed by a slave of the name of Felicissimus, to whom the administration of the mint had been committed, the workmen (monetarii) raised a rebellion in Rome, of so formidable a character, that they were able to fortify the Cœlian Mount, and it cost the Emperor the lives of 7000 of his troops to put down the insurrection. It seems incredible, that from such a cause such results should flow; but it must be remembered that Rome abounded with what we call "dangerous classes," ever ready to take part in a faction, and indifferent to the pretext which might afford them an opportunity of plunder. Besides, there is nothing about which the mind of the vulgar is more sensitive, than the interference of government with the coinage; and it might be easy for the guilty parties to persuade the populace, that some fraud upon them was intended. Ireland was nearly thrown into insurrection by the introduction of Wood's half-pence, though it was really a measure beneficial to the community. Coins of small size, called by collectors third brass, of which nearly the whole of the Methall find consists, were not issued from the

---

[1] Akerman, Manual, p. 191.
[2] Cohen, 5, 121 : 4, 349. He gives a table of the weights of the gold coin under Gallienus, showing how it varied from the standard.
[3] Hist. August., 2, 519.

time of Marcus Aurelius to that of Trajanus Decius, who preceded Valerian by about fifteen years. Their abundance, and the scarcity of those of a better class, may be justly considered as a proof of the increasing poverty of the treasury and the people.

Of the two legible coins of Valerian, one bears, on the reverse, the inscription ORIENS AUGG., for Augustorum, which must therefore have included his son and associate in the empire, Gallienus.[1] It was by the title of Augustus that the partner of the imperial power was designated, that of Cæsar, as of inferior dignity, being given to those who had been adopted as heirs.[2] The reverse of this coin, and of those generally which have a similar legend, exhibits the Sun under a human form, holding a whip in his hand, or sometimes a globe. From this association with the title Augustus, it follows that Oriens is not to be taken for the East, as when we read RESTITUTORI ORIENTIS on the coins of Gallienus, and with more truth on those of Aurelian, but as equivalent to Sol Oriens, the rising sun. This use of *Oriens* without a substantive seems, in classical times, to have been confined to the poets, as in the well known line of Virgil,—

"Nos ubi primus equis oriens adflavit anhelis."
Georg., 1, 250.

[1] Cohen maintains, in opposition to Eckhel, that the younger Valerian, the brother of Gallienus, had the title of Augustus, and attributes to him some coins with the legend Oriens Augg. Medailles Impériales, 4, 493. Eckhel refers to Saloninus, the son of Gallienus, and grandson of Valerian, the coins which, from the youthful features, Cohen attributes to the younger Valerian.

[2] Maximianus et Constantius Cæsares dicti sunt, quasi principum filii viri et designati augustæ majestatis heredes. Spartian Æl. Verus, c. 2.

It was a natural image by which to denote the youthful associate of power. By this use of *oriens*, as indicating the accession to imperial power, we may confirm the interpretation of a disputed passage in the Panegyric of an uncertain author on Constantine: "Tu nobiles Britannias illic oriendo fecisti," whence, as *oriundus* is commonly used in the sense of "born," the author has been supposed to assert that Constantine was a native of Britain. The army saluted him on his father's death Augustus and Imperator, which is sufficient to justify the panegyrist's use of *oriendo*, though Galerius refused to acknowledge him as more than Caesar.[1]

In this use of the rising Sun as a type of the accession to imperial power, which we first meet with in the reign of Hadrian,[2] but which is very common in the age to which our coins belong, we may perhaps trace the increasing worship of this luminary, which is one of the characteristics of the period. Solar worship, indeed, appears to lie at the foundation of all the systems of polytheism, but the original conception was overlaid among the Greeks and Romans, by poetical additions and anthropormorphic representations, and Apollo was to them rather the god of poetry and medicine, than the physical sun, though this character was not altogether obscured, *Phœbus* expressing the bright beams of the sun. But in the East, where poetry and art had not disguised the original

---

[1] Eburacum, by the Rev. C. Wellbeloved, p. 25.
[2] Cohen, Adrien, No. 128—9, with the legend HADRIANUS AUGUSTUS COS. III.

lineaments of mythology, as they had in the West, the distinct worship of the sun in his physical and cosmical character remained. Such was his worship in Rhodes, an Asiatic island. Its chief divinity, to whose honour the celebrated Colossus was raised, is called Helios or Sol, not Apollo. Syria, however, was especially the seat of this solar worship, and when Rome became infected with Syrian manners and ideas, and, according to the complaint of Juvenal (Sat. 3, 62), the Orontes flowed into the Tiber, we perceive the traces of it among the remains of Roman antiquity. The influences tending to the increase of the solar worship became still stronger after the reign of Hadrian. At the commencement of the century to which our coins belong, a high priest of the Syrian solar god Elagabalus had been raised to the empire, under the name of the deity whom he served. Alexander Severus was a Syrian, and as an omen of his future dignity[1] the sun, on the day of his birth, had appeared, with a crown of rays, over his father's house. Aurelian was most devoted to the worship of the sun. His mother is said to have been a priestess of the sun, and he erected a splendid temple to this divinity at Rome.

To the same cause I should attribute the general appearance of the radiated crown, on the heads of the emperors of this period. The original emblem of the imperator was the laurel or bay wreath of victory, and it was the policy of Augustus, and his first successors, to avoid all titles and symbols which savoured of royalty; if a radiated crown was

[1] Herodian, 5, 5—12.

allotted to them, it was after their death, and as gods, not as sovereigns.¹ Nero is said to have been the first who assumed it in his lifetime; it appears also in coins of Caligula, but only such as were struck in Greek cities. Flattery, however, soon extended it, even in Italy, to living emperors. " Horum unum (any one of your great deeds, says Pliny to Trajan, Paneg., c. 52) si præstitisset alius, illi jam dudum radiatum caput et media inter deos sedes staret." Gallienus wore it in public.² Whether considered as a mark of deification, or of solar worship, it would be equally offensive to Christians. After the time of Constantine we do not find the figure of the Sun on coins, and the radiated crown is replaced by a diadem of gems. The Sun was not an emblem of the emperor only, but also of Eternity, as appears from several of the coins in this collection.³

Although the general execution of these coins is rude, the impression of the imperial head upon some of them is very distinct. The contrast in feature between Valerian and his son Gallienus corresponds well enough with their respective characters. The strong bluff features of the father indicate the hardy warrior; the fine and delicate lineaments and elaborately curled beard of the son are characteristic of the man of elegant tastes, to

---

[1] Rasche Lex. Corona radiata. A coin of Julius Cæsar with a radiated crown is of doubtful authenticity. Morell, 1, p. 100. It appears on the head of Augustus, accompanied with Divus.

[2] "Radiatus sæpe processit," says Trebellius of Gallienus, c. 16.

[3] For example, No. 5 in Catalogue. Obv., GALLIENUS AUG., with radiated head. Rev., ÆTERN. AUG., the Sun standing, in left hand a globe.

whom the cares of empire were a burden, and who, though roused occasionally to activity, gladly returned to his dilettante pursuits of poetry and gardening. The features of Salonina are not of the Roman cast, and she is said to have been the daughter of a barbarian king;[1] while the coarse features of Marius, and his brawny neck, agree with the account, that he had worked at the forge before he was an emperor. It is not difficult, again, to trace a family likeness between Quintillus and his brother and predecessor Claudius Gothicus; but in general it must be acknowledged that we do not know the characters of these short-lived rulers sufficiently, to rely on such comparisons.

It would be very interesting, if it were practicable, to assign the numerous coins of Gallienus to their several years, but this can be done only with a few of them. The only certain chronology is derived from the mention of the tribunitial power, which was annually renewed, and but four of this collection have such marks. One is of the third year of tribunitial power, which was also that of his second consulship, though the number of the consulship is not given on our coin. It was in this year (255 A. D.), according to Eckhel, that Valerian, himself intent on the eastern war, committed the European armies to his son, to be employed against

---

[1] Treb. Poll., Hist. Aug., 2, 250. From the name Chrysogone, which she bears on Greek coins, she has been supposed to have been a native of a Greek city in Thrace or Asia. One of her coins (Cohen, 4, 464) has the singular epigraph, AUG. IN PACE, from which it has been conjectured, that she may have been a Christian, and that this coin was struck after her death. But as she holds the olive branch, it is more probably that *pax* is to be taken in the ordinary sense.

the barbarians. The second is of the fourth year of tribunitial power (A. D. 256) and third consulship. Coins of this year, though not ours, give Gallienus the title Germanicus, the indication of warfare at least, if not of victory, in Germany. The third is of the seventh year of tribunitial power (A. D. 259), when Gallienus gained victories on the Rhine and the Main, in memory of which, on one of his coins, he is represented standing in his paludamentum, between two rivers, prostrate on the ground.[1] The fourth in our collection with a date is of the sixteenth year of tribunitial power, the last of his reign.[2]

All the rest of the coins in this hoard are what are called *numi vagi*, of uncertain date, but they exhibit some things worthy of remark. The invasion of the barbarians and the insurrections of the Thirty Tyrants were not the only evils under which the empire suffered during the reign of Gallienus; pestilence, earthquake, and floods alarmed the superstitious fears of the people. To appease the gods, the Sibylline books were consulted, and sacrifices offered to Jupiter Salutaris.[3] To this

---

[1] Cohen, 4, 403.

[2] There is a type of the coins of Gallienus which has much exercised the pen of numismatists. The obverse exhibits his head, with the legend GALLIENÆ AUGUSTÆ, crowned with reed instead of laurel. This has been supposed to be a satire on his effeminacy. On the reverse is the legend UBIQUE PAX, as a satire on his government, under which the empire was distracted by war in every part. If it has been really struck in satire, it must have been by one of the Tyrants. The crown of reeds is found on a coin with the usual obverse, GALLIENUS (Cohen, 4, 440). Another coin with the inscription GALLIENÆ AUGUSTÆ, has a wreath of ears of corn round the head, and on the reverse VICTORIA AUGUSTI. Is this, too, a satire on his government as producing famine? The explanation is not probable, especially as the first mentioned coin is of gold. Cohen, 4, 416.

[3] Treb. Poll., Gallieni duo, c. 5.

excited state of feeling Eckhel refers the extraordinary number of coins with figures of the gods, which were struck in the reign of Gallienus. He gives a list of them, including nearly all the gods of the Pantheon; our collection contains coins with the figure of Jupiter Conservator, Jupiter Propugnator, Jupiter Ultor, Neptunus Conservator, Apollo Conservator, Diana Conservatrix, Liber Pater Conservator, and Mars Pacifer, besides Sol Conservator Augusti.

The next in our list is SALONINA, the wife of Gallienus, who is supposed to have been killed at the same time with her husband, before Milan. The types of her coins have an appropriate character; the divinities which occur are VESTA, VENUS VICTRIX, JUNO, REGINA, and JUNO LUCINA, with the attributes Pudicitia, Fecunditas,[1] Æquitas. Her bust on some of her coins is placed on a figure of the crescent moon. This appears to be another indication of the influence of the oriental worship of the Sun and Moon. The first head of an empress placed in this way is that of Julia Domna, the second wife of Septimus Severus, and grandaunt of Elagabalus, the high priest of the sun. Tranquillina, the wife of one of the Gordians, and Etruscilla, the wife of Decius, are represented in the same manner. Valeria, the daughter of Diocletian, and wife of Maximianus, is the last empress on whose coins this peculiarity appears.

One of the coins of Salonina exhibits an inscrip-

[1] FECUNDITAS (No. 3) has a small figure standing near her, and a cornucopiæ in her hand. It is connected, no doubt, with No. 6, JUNO LUCINA, sitting, with a flower in her right hand, and a swathed child in the left.

tion to a goddess who will hardly be found in the books of mythology, and may be heard of now for the first time by most of my hearers,—the goddess Segetia, whose name, derived from *seges*, corn, indicates that she presided over the harvest. She was not, however, altogether unknown. Pliny and Macrobius mention her,[1] and St. Augustine, in his book De Civitate Dei,[2] ridiculing the multiplicity of the heathen deities, observes, that not content with one, they had a goddess Seia to preside over the seed in the earth, Segetia over the standing corn, and Tutilina to protect the barn and the corn-rick. We may wonder why Segetia should have been honoured with a coin, rather than the classic Ceres. But Segetia and her two associates belonged to the old Italic divinities, the Dii Indigetes, whose worship long preceded that of the Greek Ceres; they were adored by the Roman people in the days of their early kings; their images were placed in the Circus,[3] and probably they were celebrated in the songs which the Fratres Arvales chanted, to implore the blessing of the gods and avert rust and mildew from the fields. Why Segetia now appears for the first time on the coinage, it is difficult to say; perhaps in that general invocation of the gods, which took place in the calamities of Gallienus' reign, this ancient deity may have been brought forward, to avert or remove the visitation of famine.

The coins of POSTUMUS, who made himself inde-

---

[1] Plin., N. H., 18, 2. Macrob., 1, 16. Pliny calls her Segesta. Tertullian calls the three goddesses, Sessia, from sero; Messia, from messis; Tutilina, from tutela. De Spectac., 1, 8.
[2] Lib. 4, c. 8.
[3] Plin., 18, 2.

pendent in Gaul during the reign of Gallienus, are remarkable for the variety of characters in which Hercules appears upon them. We find the Nemæan, the Erymanthian, the Thracian, the Libyan, and other classical names, and two, Hercules Magusanus [1] and Hercules Deusoniensis, derived from his local worship in Gaul or Germany. Our collection contains one of the latter, on which the god appears with the attributes of the club and the lion's skin, but without the temple, which is found on some coins with this inscription. Deuso, the town from which the name is derived, is supposed to be Deuz, opposite to Cologne, or Duisburg. As Postumus was engaged in successful wars on the Rhine with the Germans, these coins may have been struck on occasion of some victory gained on this spot. Another inscription peculiar to the coins of Postumus and his contemporary Aureolus [2] is that of CONCORDIA EQUITUM. The type is singular in both, — a female with her foot upon the prow of a vessel. Such inscriptions are evidences of the existence of Discord, and belong to times of divided authority and disputed right. We find them only in the decline of the empire. The gold coins of Postumus are very finely executed,[3] but his third brass, to which class all of this find belong, exhibit no superiority to the rest of the hoard.

The coins of VICTORINUS, who was first the colleague and afterwards the successor for a year of

---

[1] Magusani Herculis fanum pagus Scaldiæ insulæ est, hodie *Westcappel*. Rasche.

[2] Cohen, 5, 79, says, there are no genuine coins of Aureolus.

[3] A gold medallion of Postumus, formerly in the Cabinet of France, which was stolen and melted down in 1831, is valued by Cohen at 2,500 fr.

Postumus, present nothing remarkable. Though the coins of Marius, the sword-cutler who succeeded Victorinus, are not very numerous, yet as Rasche reckons up thirty-five different types, it is not very credible that he should have reigned only three days, as the Augustan historian tells us.[1]

The coins of TETRICUS the elder are, on the other hand, very numerous, as might be expected, since he retained his power not only during the reign of Claudius Gothicus, but during a considerable part of that of Aurelian. The most remarkable of them is that which is inscribed CONSECRATIO, indicating his apotheosis after death. This posthumous honour, which Julius Cæsar first enjoyed, was conferred on deceased emperors by the authority of the Senate, and is variously indicated on coins, by an eagle, as the emblem of Jupiter, in the case of an emperor, or a peacock, the bird of Juno, of an empress, or an altar, as a symbol of sacrifice, or a *thensa*, the sacred vehicle in which the images of the gods were carried in procession, or the thunderbolt of Jupiter, or a Victory, winged, and carrying the soul of the deceased to Olympus. The compliment was paid with little discrimination, Claudius, Commodus, Caracalla, Gallienus, having received it, no less than Augustus, Trajan, and the Antonines. Eckhel spoke doubtfully of the consecration of Tetricus,[2] but there is one in the Methall find which has his head on the obverse, and on the reverse *Consecratio*, with the figure of an eagle.[3]

---

[1] Hist. Aug., 2, p. 264.
[2] Doctrina Num., vol. 7, pt. 2, p. 457.
[3] The type is the same as that given by Cohen, Tetricus Père, No. 51.

The same find contains several *Consecrations* of
CLAUDIUS GOTHICUS, some with the altar, some
with the eagle. The practice ceased, of course,
with the establishment of Christianity, and few
sovereigns have since been advanced to the rank of
Saints.

There is nothing particular to be observed respecting the coins of QUINTILLUS, the brother, and
AURELIAN, the successor, of Claudius Gothicus.

Looking over the whole series, which comprehends
only seventeen years, one cannot but be struck
with the great variety of types, so unlike the
monotony of modern coinage. Of the seventy coins
of Gallienus in the Methall find, more than half
are different, and the whole number of varieties
of his coinage, of all sizes and metals, as enumerated
by Cohen, amounts to 865. If the Romans were
inferior to the Greeks in poetical genius, they
certainly far surpassed them in fertility of allegory;
indeed a great deal of what is commonly called
their religion was nothing but allegory. It is
remarkable, however, how little we know in detail
of the operations of their mint,—who were their
designers, or how their coins were executed. Classical Latinity has no name for the die in which
they were struck, and the numismatists have been
obliged to use the word *matrix* as a substitute.
Considering the immense number of types, it is
remarkable how few of these dies have been found.
Moneta, when personified (or the Monetæ, representing gold, silver, and brass), holds usually a pair
of scales, or a cornucopiæ, and has either a mass of
uncoined metal, or a heap of coins, at her feet.

The denarius of Carisius, a monetary triumvir under Augustus,[1] exhibits, besides the pileus of Vulcan, an anvil, a hammer, and a pair of tongs, but gives no information as to the die. Caylus (Rec. d' Ant., 1, 284) describes two metallic dies for striking the obverse of coins of the emperor Augustus, found at Nismes. The analysis of the metal proved them to be composed of equal portions of copper, zinc, tin, and lead. Their shape is conical, and they appear to have been placed in a collar to preserve their form under the blow of the hammer by which the impression was given. Two others of iron, described by him, represent, one, the obverse of a coin of Constantius Chlorus, the other, the reverse of a coin of Macrinus. The preparation of the die of the higher class of coins must have been the work of first-rate designers. One of these, mentioned by Eckhel, is of brass; if this was generally the case, as they could not last long, the great variety is naturally accounted for. The practice of casting coins in a mould also prevailed; a specimen is preserved in the York Museum.[2] It is remarkable that none have hitherto been found older than the time of Severus, when the silver coinage began to be debased. Whether these moulds were used by forgers, or by the officers of government for expedition, is a point on which antiquaries are not agreed.[3]

The coins of Valerian, Gallienus, Claudius Gothicus, Aurelian, who were really Emperors of *Rome*,

---

[1] Morell, Thes. Num., 5, 72.
[2] Descriptive Account of Antiquities, p. 90.
[3] Mr. King, Ancient Gems, p. 210, thinks they were not used by forgers.

would probably be struck there. Gaul had in this age three mints, one at Arles, one at Lyons, and one at Treves; and Postumus and Tetricus, who were sovereigns in Gaul, would, of course, use them. There is no trace of any mint in Britain at this time. We can hardly believe that Carausius, who maintained himself here so long in an independent dominion, whose coinage is so varied, and one of whose coins exhibits Britannia welcoming him with the words, "EXPECTATE VENI," had not a mint of his own,[1] but we have no positive proof of it. The coins of Constantine, inscribed PLON., are generally referred to a London mint; and perhaps Londinium, as a great seat of commerce, was better entitled to this distinction than the military capital, Eburacum. The honour of having a special mint, York seems to owe to her Northumbrian Sovereigns.[2]

[1] Cohen, who reckons 276 types of Carausius, says, "Toutes ses medailles ont été frappées en Angleterre."

[2] See a paper by R. Davies, Esq., F. S. A., in Proceedings of Yorkshire Philosophical Society, p. 191.

IV.

THE CAUSES OF THE DESTRUCTION OF CLASSICAL LITERATURE.

ALTHOUGH subjects purely literary are not regarded as belonging to the province of this Society, the connexion of Literature with History is clearly within its limits. This connexion is of the most intimate kind. The relation of the world in which we live to those of Greece and Rome, has been chiefly determined by the transmission of their literature to our times. Had their books all perished, the material antiquities which might have come down to us, their sculpture and architecture, their coins, their weapons of war, their domestic furniture, would have given us a very imperfect conception of the twelve or fourteen centuries which elapsed from Homer to the downfall of the Western Empire. We might have learnt their stature from their skeletons, their physiognomy from their busts, the outward forms of their religion from the sculptures of their temples, their altars, and their sarcophagi, and the mythological emblems on their coins. Their arms and their military roads and works would have shewn us something of their system of offensive and defensive warfare; but the *mind* of the Greek and Roman people would have escaped us; for *that* lives only in books. Nor is it only their own history that would have been lost to us. What should we have known of the rest of the ancient world, but for the light reflected upon it from the pages of the Greek and Roman historians? The transmission of the writings of the great masters of Grecian thought has made us what we are, in intellectual and moral philosophy, in taste, and even in science. Had the Codes of Roman Law perished in the destruction of the Western Empire, we should have lost the benefit of the long succession of labours, by which the system of Jurisprudence had been perfected. It will, therefore, I hope, be an interesting subject to enquire, what portion of classical literature perished in that great convulsion, what portion escaped, and to what causes its partial recovery is to be attributed. For while there is not one department of ancient literature that has not suffered by the loss of eminent writers, there is hardly one in which the destruction has been total.

The fortunes of books in ancient times must have depended very much upon those of public libraries. The art of printing has furnished every house in England, inhabited by a family in circumstances of competence, with a library, comprising, at least, the principal classics of our own language. We cannot conceive of conflagrations, or floods, or civil convulsions, which should destroy every copy of Shakespeare, Milton, or Goldsmith, of Robinson Crusoe or John Bunyan, of Hume's or Gibbon's Histories. Even the burning down of the Bodleian or the British Museum, though it would be mourned over by the bibliographer, whose delight is in rare and unique copies, would scarcely involve the extinction of a single author of any value to posterity. It was far otherwise in ancient times. The Athenians were not a book-learned people. They learnt Homer from the recitations of the rhapsodists; Æschylus and Sophocles from the theatre; they heard Pericles and Demosthenes thundering in the agora; they picked up their philosophy in the portico or the garden of Academus. Polycrates of Samos is said to have collected a large library,[1] but we hear little of libraries at Athens till near the close of her time of independence. There is, indeed, a story, which rests only on late authority,[2] that Pisistratus founded a public library at Athens, which was subsequently increased by the Athenian people, and which Xerxes carried away to Persia, whence Seleucus Nicanor, more than a century and a half later, obtained it and restored it to Athens. But I am more inclined to adopt the statement of Strabo,[3] who says, that Aristotle was the first collector of a library, to which no doubt the munificence of his royal pupil contributed. This library he left to Theophrastus, his successor at the Lyceum. The Macedonian Kings of Egypt, following the advice of Aristotle, formed libraries strictly public. Their predecessors, the Pharaohs, had set them the example. Osymandyas, according to Diodorus,[4] collected a large library at Thebes, and inscribed over the door characters signifying "The Repository of Medicine for the Mind." Champollion, in his Letters from Egypt, professes to have found, among

[1] Athen., 1, 3.
[2] Gellius, 6, 17, Lipsius de Bibliothecis (Op. 6, p. 1123), and Hospinian de Bibliothecis, contain much information concerning ancient libraries.
[3] Lib. 13, p. 608. Ed. Casaub.
[4] Hist. 1, c. 41.

the ruins of the Ramesseion, a hall, over the door of which was a figure of a goddess, who bears the title of "Mistress of Letters, presiding over the Hall of Books."[1] The example of the first Ptolemy was followed by his successors. They collected the autograph works of eminent authors, when it was possible to obtain them, or procured copies. The abundance and cheapness of the papyrus in Egypt enabled them to do this, with less expence than must have been incurred by other collectors. The first of these Alexandrian libraries was established in the Brucheium, the quarter of the royal palace where was also the Museum, inhabited by the learned men, who pursued their studies under the patronage of the Ptolemies, and were admitted to their society.[2] It is related of Ptolemy Euergetes (III.), that when the Athenians were suffering from a dearth of corn, he would not allow them to be supplied from the granaries of Alexandria, unless they would send him the works of Æschylus, Sophocles, and Euripides, for transcription.[3] I am sorry to say that even in those days book-collectors were not strictly conscientious. Ptolemy kept the autographs, and sent back the copies, being content to forfeit the deposit of fifteen talents, by which the Athenians had hoped to secure the return of the originals.

The increasing number of Jews in Alexandria[4]

---

[1] Lettres d' Egypte, p. 285. The reader should be informed that, according to Champollion's colleague, Rosellini, these letters, written for the Parisian public, are not always to be relied upon. Monumenti del Culto, p. 353.

[2] Strabo, 18, p. 794.

[3] Galen, Comm. ad Hippocr., lib. 3.

[4] Joseph. Bell. Jud., 2, 18, 7.

drew the attention of the founder of the Library, and induced him, it is said, to dispatch an embassy to Jerusalem, requesting that men might be sent to him, competent to translate their Law into Greek. Accordingly seventy-two were sent, who were shut up in separate cells, and produced an equal number of versions, all agreeing in every single word,—an unanimity which since that time no two translators have ever attained.[1] The story savours strongly of Jewish credulity and exaggeration; but it is not improbable that a copy of the Jewish Law in Greek, may have been placed among the multifarious contents of the Alexandrian library.[2] The Bruchcium was insufficient to contain them all, and a second library was formed in the Serapeum,[3] or temple of Serapis, in one of the suburbs. It was the former which was destroyed in the conflagration kindled by Cæsar's soldiers, in the Alexandrian war. Antony, to gratify Cleopatra,[4] in some measure repaired the loss, by transferring hither the library of the kings of Pergamus, amounting to 200,000 volumes. They, too, had

---

Apion, 2, 4. Ant., 12, 1, 14, 7, 19, 5, 2. They had their own quarter, their own Ethnarch, their own temple, the Oneion, and formed, in fact, an independent community.

[1] Joseph. Ant., 12, 2. Euseb. Præp. Evang., 13, 12. The letter of Aristeas, on which the story rests, is generally admitted to be an Alexandrian forgery.

[2] Jerome (Quæst. sup. Trad. Hebr.) assigns a special reason for Ptolemy's desire to have a copy of the Hebrew Scriptures. "Judæos ille Platonis sectator magni iccirco faciebat, quia unum Deum colere dicerentur." If Tertullian (Apologeticus, c. 18) may be believed, the Hebrew original was extant in his time in the Serapeum.

[3] Ammian. Marcell., 22, 15, erroneously describes the library in the Serapeum as burnt. The Bruchcium adjoined the docks and harbour.

[4] Plut., Vit. M. Antonii, c. 58, 7. According to Vitruvius (7 ad init) they had preceded the Ptolemies as book collectors.

been book collectors,¹ and the Ptolemies, through jealousy, had forbidden the exportation of the papyrus. The use of prepared skins (διφθέραι) for writing upon, had been immemorial in Asia.¹ The chronicles of the kingdom of Persia, which Ahasuerus read on that sleepless night,² which saved the Jewish people from massacre, were written on this material; for Ctesias, who wrote a History of Persia, tells us that he had compiled it from "royal skins." The name retains the trace of its local origin, for *parchment* is but a corruption of *pergament*. The Brucheium is said to have numbered 700,000 volumes.³ These figures are startling; but it must be remembered, that each division of a work, in ancient times, was written on a separate roll (volumen), so that Homer was in forty-eight volumes, Herodotus in nine, and so on. Making allowance for this mode of reckoning, and for possible exaggeration, it will still be probable, that the Alexandrian libraries contained copies of every production of Greek literature, published before the conquest of Egypt by the Romans.

The history of Aristotle's library will shew how early the destruction of classical literature began.⁴ He left it to Theophrastus, his successor at the Lyceum. The books came afterwards by inheritance into the hands of illiterate persons at Scepsis, who were apprehensive that they might be seized by the kings of Pergamus, who possessed Scepsis,

---

¹ Herod., 5, 58.
² Esther, 6, 1. Ctesias, as quoted by Diod., Sic. 2, 32.
³ Gellius, 6, 7. Seneca De Tranq., c. 9, reckons them at 400,000. Ammianus Marcellinus, 22, 16, agrees with Gellius.
⁴ Strabo, 13, p. 609.

and to prevent this they buried them in a vault, where they experienced the same fate which has befallen many of our public records; they were rotted by damp, and gnawed by worms. When the danger was passed, they were brought out, and sold for a large sum to Apellicon of Teos, whom Strabo describes as "a lover of books rather than a lover of wisdom." He troubled himself little about the purity of the text, but was anxious to bring his MSS. into a saleable condition, and filled up the gaps without knowledge or judgment. Sylla brought them to Rome, and consigned them to the charge of Tyrannion, a grammarian, and follower of Aristotle, but he allowed them to be copied by booksellers, who employed ignorant scribes, and the transcripts were put in circulation without revision or correction. The reader of Aristotle has often cause to regret that the philosopher was so sparing of his words, and may be excused if he sometimes bestows a malediction on the worms; but his worst enemy has been the faithless transcriber, who has substituted his own words for those of Aristotle, and thus cheated him with a false appearance of meaning.[1] There were other sources of loss and corruption. Galen, in the middle of the second century after Christ, speaking particularly of medical books, says that "many authors did not publish their works during their lifetime; so that only one, or at most two, copies existing, they were easily lost; some also were suppressed by those who wished to claim as novelties

---

[1] Twining's Translation of the Poetic of Aristotle. Pref., p. 7.

the discoveries of their predecessors; and others, again, perished by conflagrations or earthquakes."[1]

When books were multiplied only by transcription, the entire loss of such authors as Galen refers to was more likely to occur than in modern times. But I believe that at Rome, at least, the lighter kinds of literature were pretty extensively diffused, and that there was not that wide difference in expence which is commonly supposed between a written and a printed copy. Martial, in the 118th Epigram of his first book,[2] is addressing an economical friend, Lupercus, who had proposed to send his boy to borrow from Martial a copy of his work, with a promise to return it as soon as read. Martial tells him, that it would be a pity to give the boy the trouble to mount to the garret in which he lived; that there was a shop kept by Atrectus in the Forum, with posts on each side the door, (the reader of Pope will remember "Lintot's rubric post,") inscribed with the titles of all the Latin poets, and that for five denarii the bookseller would hand him down, from the first or second pigeonhole (nidus), a copy of Martial "pumice rasum purpuraque cultum," or, as we should say, "hot-pressed and with illuminated letters." Now five denarii would be hardly 3s. 6d. "You will say, The book is not worth so much." "You are a wise man,

---

[1] Comm. de Nat. Hom., quoted by Villoison, Proleg. Hom., p. 37.

[2] Professor Norton, (Genuineness of the Gospels, 1, 31) quoting this epigram of Martial, infers from it the probability that there would be 60,000 copies of the Gospels in the hands of the Christians of the second century. He has forgotten, I think, the low state of learning among them, even at a later date, as indicated by the inscriptions in the Catacombs.

Lupercus." And this was evidently a copy for the drawing room table. On common paper, and without illuminations, the price would probably have been one half less. In the imperial times a library was the fashionable appendage of a wealthy house. Seneca complains (De Tranq., c. 9) that books were bought "non in studium sed in spectaculum," and as the "cænationum ornamenta." Pliny had a single bookcase in his Laurentian Villa (Ep. 2, 17), but it contained choice authors, "non legendos sed lectitandos," to be perused and re-perused.

Books were among the spoils which Roman generals brought from conquered states; Æmilius Paulus from Macedonia, Lucullus from Pontus. In the foundation of public libraries Asinius Pollio [1] led the way. Julius Cæsar, had he lived, would have founded a library of Greek and Latin books, and placed the celebrated antiquary, Varro, at the head of it.[2] Augustus deposited a large collection of Greek and Latin books in the Temple of the Palatine Apollo,[3] and another in the Portico of Octavia, near the Theatre of Marcellus.[4] The fashion thus set was followed, and Tiberius[5] and Vespasian both founded libraries, the latter in the Temple of Peace.[6] In the conflagration of the city under Nero the imperial palace on the Palatine was built, and, no doubt, when Tacitus[7] mentions, among the treasures which were destroyed, not

[1] Plin., 35, 2. Isidor. Hisp., 6, 4.
[2] Sueton, J. Cæs., c. 44.
[3] Sueton, Octav., c. 29; Gram., 20. Hyginus, his freedman, was the first librarian.
[4] Sueton, Gram., 21.
[5] Gellius, 13, 19. It was used by Vopiscus, Probus, c. 2.
[6] Gellius, 5, 21.
[7] Ann., 15, 38.

only "artium decora," but "monumenta ingeniorum antiqua et incorrupta," he must mean by the latter, books. The fire which took place when the Vitellians attacked the Capitol was very destructive: Domitian endeavoured to repair the losses caused by it and the fire under Nero, by sending transcribers abroad, and especially to Alexandria, to make copies of the works preserved there.[1] Trajan built a new Forum, and among its public buildings was a library, called from him Bibliotheca Ulpia. The Temple of Hercules at Tivoli was furnished with a library, probably placed there by Hadrian. It contained the works of Aristotle.[2] Publius Victor, in his work De Regionibus Urbis, enumerates 29 libraries in Rome, but the age and even genuineness of this work have been called in question by Bunsen and Becker. The younger Gordian, A. D. 237, is the last emperor who is said to have founded a library in Rome. It consisted of 62,000 volumes and had been bequeathed by his preceptor Serenus Sammonicus, a wealthy man of letters.[3]

We have little information respecting the libraries of the provincial towns; but the emperors, particularly Antoninus Pius, took great pains to diffuse knowledge, by establishing schools of rhetoric, philosophy, Greek and Latin literature, in the great cities. Milan, Lyons, Marseilles, Carthage, were, to speak in modern language, provincial universities.[4]

[1] Sueton, Dom. 20.
[2] Gellius, 19, 5.
[3] J. Capitolinus, Gordianus Junior, c. 18.
[4] See Heeren, Geschichte der Classischen Litteratur, 1, 20. To this work of the learned Professor of Göttingen, whose lectures I had the advantage of attending in the winter of 1819 —20, I have to acknowledge myself much indebted.

Their studies could not be carried on without collections of books, and from these, subsequently dispersed and preserved in monasteries, probably many works, recovered at the revival of letters, were derived. When Constantinople was founded, the new capital was not left destitute of public libraries. The first was said to have been founded by Constantius, the son of Constantine the Great, but it was much enlarged and enriched by Julian. The historians of the Church have branded him with the name of Apostate; but he was a zealous patron of letters, and especially industrious in the collection of books. "Some" he says, in one of his Epistles, "are fond of horses, some of birds, some of wild beasts, but from my boyhood I have had a most passionate eagerness for the acquisition of books."[1] His literary tastes, so rare among the emperors since the Antonines, had no doubt something to do with his return to the old religion, under whose influence Greek and Latin literature had been produced. He added his own library to that of Constantius, and together the books amounted to 120,000.[2]

From the account which has now been given, it is evident, that had not that great convulsion occurred, which we call the irruption of the Barbarians, the inheritance of Greek and Roman learning might have descended to us with little diminution. But such was not the plan of Divine Providence.

---

[1] Epist. ad Ecdicium. A library which he had formed at Antioch was destroyed by his successor Jovian, after it had been much injured by the petulance of the people of Antioch. Suidas, Jovianus. Gibbon, c. 24, note 128.

[2] Zosimus, 2, 11. Themist., 68, 13.

In the course of the fifth century Rome was thrice sacked; once by Alaric and his Goths, once by Genseric and his Vandals, and again by Ricimer. The Goths and the Vandals have had the stigma fixed upon them of being the destroyers of ancient literature as well as art. Pope, in a well known line, joins Gothic fire with Papal piety,[1] as authors of the mischief. A fire kindled in a great city burns indiscriminately whatever it meets with; but books are no special objects of the cupidity of soldiers, and, indeed, according to Zonaras, the Gothic troops were advised by one of their chiefs to leave the Athenians their books, which, like a true barbarian, he regarded as some of those instruments of luxury, which had corrupted military virtue, and made them an easy prey.[2] He would have predicted a speedy decay to a country that had established regimental libraries. The Gothic chiefs remonstrated with Amalasuntha for having the heir of the monarchy placed under a schoolmaster.

The Lombards, in the sixth century, carried destruction with them in the course of their conquests. Gregory the Great, who witnessed them, says, they sacked cities, burnt churches, destroyed monasteries, and made countries previously teeming with population, deserts through which wild beasts passed.[3]

From the fifth century to the Revival of Letters it is to the Latin Church that we must look for the preservation of the Latin classics. The allusion

---

[1] Epistle to Addison.
[2] Gibbon, ch. 10, 1, p. 434. He doubts the truth of the anecdote, apparently without reason. It is given by Zonaras, 12, 26. Procop. de Bell. Goth., c. 11.
[3] Dial., 3, c. 38.

in Pope's "papal piety" is to a story found in the Nugæ Curialium of Joannes Sarisberiensis, a writer of the twelfth century. Speaking of Gregory the Great, who sat on the papal throne from 590 to 604, he says, "that it was reported that he burnt the Palatine library, in order that the grace of God might have freer scope."[1] The story may be doubtful, as Tiraboschi earnestly maintains;[2] but the *animus* of Gregory towards classical literature displays itself very plainly, in a letter which he wrote to Desiderius, Bishop of Vienne, who, he had heard, devoted himself to classical studies, and read heathen poets.[3] "The praises of Jupiter and of Christ cannot go together in the same mouth, and it is for you to consider, what a gross impiety it is for a bishop to repeat, what is unsuitable even for a religious layman."[4] One who thought thus of classical books was not unlikely to have burnt them, and could not consistently encourage their preservation. His own Latin style is barbarous, and he glories in setting aside the rules of Donatus.[5]

---

[1] 2, 26. "Doctor sanctissimus Gregorius non modo mathesin jussit ab aula recedere sed, ut traditur a majoribus, incendio dedit probatæ lectionis, Scripta Palatinus quæcumque tenebat Apollo, in quibus erant præcipue quæ cælestium mentem et superiorum oracula videbantur hominibus revelare." *Mathesis* is evidently astrology.

[2] Storia, 3, 101—113. Another imputation upon him is, that he suppressed as far as possible, from pious motives, the works of Cicero and Livy. Bayle, no lover of popes, is inclined to acquit him of all the charges.

[3] Ep., 9, 48. Heeren thinks that what Gregory burnt were only the books of the Cumæan Sibyl, which Augustus, after destroying a great many others, carefully preserved in the Temple of the Palatine Apollo. They had a narrow escape in a fire in the reign of Julian. Amm. Marc., 23, 3.

[4] "Quid facit cum psalterio Horatius, cum evangeliis Maro, cum apostolis Cicero?" St. Jerome ad Eustochium. In his unsaintly days Jerome had made himself perfectly acquainted with the Latin classics.

[5] Dedic. Moral. ad Leandrum.

The northern hive was not the only source from which the destroyers of classical literature issued forth. The seventh century witnessed the rise of Islam, and Alexandria was taken by the Saracens in the first century of the Hejra. I have already mentioned the losses which its great library had sustained in the wars of Cæsar and Antony. The Temple of Serapis had been a safeguard to the books which it contained, while the worship of Serapis lasted; but having lost its sanctity, it became a place of danger. In the 28th chapter of Gibbon's History we have a detailed account of the attack made by the people of Alexandria, headed by their bishop, Theophilus, on the Temple of Serapis, in which the pagans had taken refuge. It was stormed and levelled with the ground, and the library, no doubt, perished in the flames. Alexandria, however, still continued to be a seat of Greek learning, and though its royal libraries had been destroyed, there appears no sufficient ground to doubt, that a great conflagration of books took place, when Amrou, the general of the Caliph Omar, reduced it. The reply of Omar, when consulted as to the fate of the books, "that if they agreed with the Qoraun they were useless, and if they differed from it they were pernicious," seems to me too characteristic to have been invented. When Gibbon wrote, no older authority was known for the story of their destruction and their number, which sufficed to heat the baths of Alexandria for six months, than the Christian bishop Abulpharagius, who lived in the thirteenth century; it has since been found that Abdollatif, an Egyptian physician of the twelfth century,[1] gives the same account. After a while fanaticism subsided, and the Caliphs of Bagdad became liberal patrons of literature and science, and this continued to be the character of the Mahommedan rulers, till the Turks introduced a worse barbarism than that of the first followers of the prophet.

From this time Constantinople must be considered as the City of Refuge for Greek literature. Here it was safe from barbarian hands, but not from fire and earthquake and faction. The capital was the scene of incessant outbreaks, sometimes produced by the rivalry of the greens and blues, the parties of the circus; sometimes by religious dissensions; sometimes by political insurrections; and the populace had the habit, which the Turks seem to have inherited from them, of expressing their ill-humour by setting fire to the city. In one of these, in the reign of Basiliscus, in the fifth century, Julian's library of 120,000 volumes was consumed.[2] In the disturbances occasioned by the Iconoclastic controversy, in the eighth century, a public library of many thousand volumes was consumed.[3] The monks were generally favourable to the use of images; they were consequently persecuted by the Iconoclastic emperors, who destroyed the convents and their contents.

Yet, as compared with its present state, Greek literature in that age was rich indeed. We have

---

[1] Published by Paulus in his Compendium Memorabilium Ægypti.
[2] Heeren, 1, 35.
[3] Heeren, 1, 88, is inclined to call the fact in question, which is attested first by Cedrenus who lived in the eleventh century, and was a compiler of little judgment.

the means of forming some idea of its extent, from the *Myriobiblon* of Photius.[1] He is best known by his title of Patriarch of Constantinople, but he began life as Chief Secretary, an office to which judicial functions were attached, and was afterwards Protospatharius, Captain or Colonel of the Life Guards, and ambassador from the Emperor of Constantinople to the court of one of the Caliphs. He was a man of extraordinary vigour of mind, of encyclopædical knowledge, and so devoted to reading, that he is said to have passed whole nights without sleep.[2] Not being disposed to intermit his studies while on his embassy, he carried with him an ample library. He had a brother, Tarasius, to whom he dedicates his Myriobiblon, a collection of extracts and abstracts of the authors which he had read. "Having been appointed," he says, "by the Senate and the Emperor to the Assyrian embassy, I have desired, my dearest brother, to send you abstracts of the books at whose reading you have not been present, both that you might be consoled for my absence, and that you might acquire at least a general knowledge of the authors read in your absence. In number they are 279."[3] Gibbon is inclined to doubt whether Photius could have carried such a library with him. It must, indeed, have been a "load of many camels," but we know from Indian experience, with what a train great

---

[1] Fabric. Bibl. Gr., 5, 38.

[2] Nicetas Paphlagon, in Vita Ignatii. Ignatius was the Patriarch of Constantinople, deposed by the emperor Michael III. to make way for the elevation of Photius.

[3] Procem. ad fratrem Tarasium. From the conclusion it appears that he had intended his work to include 315 authors, and he promises, if he returned from his embassy, to continue the work.

men travel in the East.[1] Nor must we form our idea of what Photius was likely to do, from the outfit of a modern ambassador, setting out for St. Petersburgh or Vienna, in which we should probably not find 300 volumes of any kind, certainly not such volumes as Photius read,—History, Divinity, and Philosophy. They served him, no doubt, for recreation on his journeys, which would be slow, and we know not how long his embassy lasted; but his diligence is astonishing, the Myriobiblon forming, with the Latin translation, a folio volume of 1,500 pages. I have introduced the mention of Photius and his embassy, in order to give an idea of what the extent of the Greek classical library was in his day. Several authors, Ctesias and Conon,[2] are known only by his extracts, and many others were read by him in their integrity, of whom now only portions remain. The history of Diodorus Siculus, which is now imperfect from the fifth book to the eleventh, and from the twentieth to the fortieth, was then complete in forty books, beginning with the fabulous times, and ending with Cæsar's wars in Gaul.[3] The same was the case with Polybius, of whose forty books only five are entire, the rest existing in fragments and an Epitome. The Roman History of Dionysius of Halicarnassus was then complete in twenty books;[4] we have only eleven entire, with fragments of the rest, partly preserved in extracts made in the tenth century by

---

[1] St. Jerome carried with him his library, which must have been, at least, as large as that of Photius, from Rome to Bethlehem.

[2] Conon wrote a collection of fifty mythical narratives, which Photius has condensed.

[3] Phot., c. 70.

[4] Phot., c. 83.

command of the Emperor Constantine Porphyrogenitus. Of the twenty-four books of Appian, one half appear to have perished. Theopompus, whom the ancient critics ranked as second in historical merit to Herodotus and Thucydides, was even then imperfect; five out of fifty-eight books of his History of Philip of Macedon had been long lost,[1] or at least were not in the library of Photius. WE have lost the whole, not only of this, but of his other historical works.

Several sections of the Myriobiblon are devoted to the Greek orators,[2] among whom Time has made even greater havoc. Thirty-five orations of Antiphon, with whom the history of Greek oratory begins, of unquestioned genuineness, were then extant; they are now reduced to fifteen. Of the sixty-five genuine orations of Demosthenes, which Photius read, we have only sixty-one; we may less regret that only thirty-four have escaped of 233 of Lysias; eleven of the fifty of Isæus; one of the fifty-two of Hyperides, and even that is of doubtful authenticity.[3]

These figures, however, give us an imperfect idea of the literary treasures which Constantinople contained in that age. This was only a portable library. Photius was a man of wealth and a collector, so that, according to the expression of Nicetas,[4] he

---

[1] Phot., c. 176.
[2] Phot., c. 259—268.
[3] Spurious orations, it appears from Photius, had been fathered upon almost all the Greek orators. Many of them had been probably exercises and declamations in schools of rhetoric, ascribed by mistake, rather than fraud, to those in whose names they were composed. From the same cause spurious orations seem to have intruded themselves among the works of Cicero.
[4] See p. 143, note 2.

was inundated with a deluge of books; yet his private library cannot have contained everything. We have other proofs how great our losses have been. The succeeding age at Constantinople, the tenth century after Christ, was that of the Lexicographers and Scholiasts, a class of writers who always make their appearance in the evening twilight of letters. We must not, however, allow ourselves to speak ungratefully of them or of the Anthologists. We cannot open a volume of the Attic writers, especially the dramatists, without finding a large appendix of fragments, preserved by the Lexicographers and Scholiasts, not for their beauty, of which they were insensible, but for grammatical or exegetical commentary. We are inclined to envy them the possession of the entire jewels, of which the sparks are so precious.

The Byzantine sovereigns of the tenth and eleventh centuries were, for the most part, patrons, and some cultivators, of letters.[1] Constantine Porphyrogenitus reigned during the first half of the tenth century. With the view of surrounding himself with able men for the discharge of public functions, he took special care that they should be trained in rhetoric and philosophy, then considered as the two great elements of a statesman's education. He made them his companions, encouraged the most promising by pecuniary rewards, and, in due time, advanced them to be judges, senators, and provincial governors. He was a collector of books, which he brought together from all parts. But he probably was indirectly the cause of the neglect

[1] Heeren, 1, 149.

and ultimate loss of many of the classic authors, especially of the historians. He says of himself, that having perceived the immense mass of books to be overpowering to the readers, he had caused abridgments to be made of them. The natural consequence of this was, that the bulky originals were neglected for these more compendious forms, and ceased to be transcribed.

The Lexicographers and Scholiasts, and authors of abridgments and selections, pursued their labours with great diligence during the eleventh century, but all creative genius, and all purity of taste, had vanished from the Eastern Empire. This century produced two female authors, phænomena more rare in ancient times than in our own; and both were of imperial rank. One of these was the princess Eudocia, the wife of Constantine XI., and after his death of Romanus IV. To him she dedicates the work which, with feminine elegance, she calls a Violet Bed *(Ionia)*. It is a mere compilation of mythological stories, with a few biographical anecdotes. Her violets have been dried in blotting paper, and have lost their native colour and fragrance.[1] The other imperial authoress is better known, the princess Anna Comnena, one of a family which, as long as they retained the throne, were steady patrons of learning. Anna is known not very favourably, to English readers, from the part assigned to her by Sir Walter Scott in Count

---

[1] In imitation, perhaps, of the Empress, Macarius Chrysocephalus, archbishop of Philadelphia, in the fourteenth century, composed his *Rhodonia* (Rosegarden), a collection of extracts from Greek authors of various ages. See Villoison, Anecd. Græca, 2, 1—79.

Robert of Paris, who, as Lockhart confesses, has taken some liberties with her character on very slight foundation, and has made an unmerciful display of the vanity, pedantry, and bad taste by which her talents were alloyed. Yet among the Byzantine historians she shines as a genius, and if her Alexiad is rather a panegyric than a biography of her father, it is a venial fault in a daughter, who sincerely admired and affectionately loved him. He is the Alexius of the First Crusade, so bitterly complained of by the Latin historians of that expedition, for his faithless conduct towards the warriors who had come to his aid. No doubt he dreaded his auxiliaries, at least as much as he did the Turks, and availed himself of those artifices which are the natural resource of the weak, and which had long been the characteristic of the Byzantine Greeks. But we have reason to rejoice that he succeeded in keeping them out of his capital. Walter the Penniless, had he reached Constantinople, would have been sorely tempted by the sight of its riches. Godfrey of Bouillon was animated by much purer motives; but in the train of the best disciplined armies there follows a host, whose only interest in the enterprize is the hope of plunder and license. Their admission within the walls of Constantinople would have exposed its literary treasures, as well as its wealth, to imminent danger.

That this is no imaginary anticipation is proved by what actually took place in the Fourth, or what is called the Latin Crusade. The two great divisions of the Christian Church had long cherished most unchristian feelings towards each other. These feelings had not originated merely in theological differences. "In every age," says Gibbon, "the Greeks were proud of their superiority in profane and religious knowledge; they had first received the light of Christianity; they had pronounced the decrees of the seven general councils; they alone possessed the language of Scripture and philosophy; nor should the Barbarians of the West, immersed in darkness, presume to argue on the high and mysterious questions of theological science. Those Barbarians despised, in their turn, the restless and subtle levity of the Orientals, the authors of every heresy, and blessed their own simplicity, which was content to hold the tradition of the Apostolic Church." This would be an unsuitable place for entering into theological controversies, much more for attempting to decide them; but as an historical fact it may be mentioned, that since the seventh century the Latin and the Greek Churches had been at variance, respecting the Procession of the Holy Spirit, the Latins attributing a participation in it to the Son, which the Greeks denied. On this question the *odium theologicum* had developed itself, with an intensity unusual even in that virulent disease. Each party charged the other with schism, and it would be difficult to say whether a schismatic or an infidel was looked upon with the deeper abhorrence. Their animosity had been carried beyond the limits of the present world, and the popes had solemnly pronounced an anathema on the heterodox, with the usual penalty of eternal perdition. I mention these things, not to reproach the bigotry of the age, but because a knowledge of the reciprocal feelings of the Greeks and Latins is necessary, in order to understand the events of the Fourth Crusade, so eminently pernicious to classical literature.[1]

The family of the Comneni had been dispossessed of the throne, and the quarrels of Isaac Angelus with his brother had occasioned the occupation of Constantinople by Baldwin, Count of Flanders. The conquests of the First Crusade had been in great measure lost. Jerusalem had been taken by Saladin; the valour of Richard of the Lion Heart had not been able to effect more than the recovery of the sea coast, and a stipulation for undisturbed admission to the Holy Sepulchre. Innocent III. stimulated Christendom to a Fourth Crusade, and an army under Baldwin, Count of Flanders, had already reached Venice, on its way to Palestine, when he was induced to divert his course to Constantinople by Alexius, the son of Isaac Angelus, in order to assist his father in regaining the throne of which he had been deprived. At their first entrance the Venetians set fire to a whole quarter of the city; in a subsequent quarrel with some Mahometans their mosch was burnt, and a conflagration arose which lasted two days and nights,

---

[1] The antagonism of the Churches shews itself in a ludicrous way in the picture which Nicetas draws of the Patriarch of Venice, who took possession of the see of Constantinople after the Latin conquest. "He was of middle size, and his figure that of a fatted hog; the surface of his face was shorn of hair, like the rest of that race, and even the hair of his breast was carefully taken off by a depilatory plaster; his dress was tightly fastened to his skin, and sewed to his wrists; he had a ring on his hand, and leather protectors, divided at the fingers, upon his hands." De Signis, c. 1. Sleeves and trowsers were, to the Greeks and Romans, marks of the Barbarians.

and spread so widely, that a Byzantine historian declares, that all the fires the city had suffered were not to be compared with it. A third fire, accompanying the sack of the city, began where the second had ended. It was not merely the dwellings of the common people that suffered, but public buildings, churches, convents, and palaces,[1] in which the most valuable repositories of books were to be found. The armies of the later Crusaders were made up of the refuse of society in the West; the pious zeal of the associates of Godfrey had given place to the mere spirit of adventure; and no cruelties practised by Christian on infidel, or infidel on Christian, could surpass those which the orthodox Latin inflicted on the schismatic Greek.[2] In addition to this source of hatred, they despised the Byzantines as a race of unwarlike penmen, and carried about books, the spoil of their libraries, with reed pens and ink bottles, in derision of their literary occupations.[3] To the ravages of fire and barbarism in this war, I think we must attribute the circumstance that so many works read by Photius in the ninth century, and by the Lexicographers and

[1] The trophies of this pillage are found in various parts of the West. The Treasury of St. Denis was enriched by a piece of the true cross, some of the "cheveux de N. S. qu'il ot en son enfance," his swaddling clothes, a thorn from his crown, a piece of the scarlet robe put on him in mockery, and a rib and tooth of St. Philip; all taken by Baldwin from the chapel of the emperor. Recueil des Hist. des Gaules, 17, 392. The Treasury of the Collegiate Church of St. Peter and St. Stephen at Troyes contains (or did contain) agates which had formed a part of the imperial cabinet at Constantinople. The head of St. Philip, taken from the Greeks at the same time, and brought to Troyes by the Grand Almoner of the French army, was deposited in a reliquary in the same church.

[2] Nicetas bitterly reproaches the Latins with committing cruelties on the people of Constantinople, from which "the Ishmaelites" had abstained when they took Jerusalem. P. 762. Ed. Bonn. His accounts are fully borne out by Villehardouin.

[3] Nicetas, p. 786.

Scholiasts, Suidas, Eustathius, Tzetzes, in the tenth, eleventh, and twelfth, had disappeared, before Greek literature was brought into the West in the fourteenth. Nothing that occurred in the interval could explain it. The family of the Palæologi, the last sovereigns of Constantinople, were patrons of learning; we read of none of those destructive conflagrations which have occurred before. The Turks plundered the city, but they did not set it on fire. As many as 120,000 volumes were lost to their owners; but as this statement is accompanied by another, that ten volumes might be purchased for a ducat, we may hope that the capture of Constantinople was the means rather of dispersing the Greek classics than of destroying them.[1] At all events, the most precious of them had reached Italy, and were there in safety.

Before we take leave of this subject we must look back on the state of Latin classical literature in the West. The age of devastation and destruction had passed, when the Northern invaders had possessed themselves of the different European kingdoms, though partially renewed by the ravages of the Danes. Classical studies could not be expected to find much favour, from a warlike aristocracy. Enlightened sovereigns, such as Charlemagne, patronized schools and collected learned men about them, but to the monasteries we chiefly owe the preservation of the Latin classics.[2] All

[1] Gibbon, chap. 67.
[2] Sidonis Apollinaris in the fifth century thus describes a conventual library (Lib. 4, 11), speaking of its founder—
Triplex bibliotheca, quo magistro,
Romana, Attica, Christiana fulsit
Quam totam monachus, virente in ævo,
Secreta bibit institutione.

churchmen were not so hostile to heathen literature as St. Gregory. A monk of the abbey of Pomposa, near Ravenna, takes a more candid view of the mixture of heathen and Christian studies. After praising his abbat for his diligence in collecting theological works, he adds, "But captious persons will ask, 'Why does the reverend abbat place heathen authors, histories of tyrants, and such books, among theological works?' To these I answer, in the words of the Apostle, 'There are vessels of clay as well as vessels of gold.' By these means the tastes of all are excited to study."[1] The copying of books was one of the occupations of the Benedictine monks, and the founder, at least, did not prohibit the copying of heathen authors. But where we gain a glance into the contents of monastic libraries in the Middle Ages, the later writers much predominate over the classics properly so called, and theology over classics altogether. The poetical description which Alcuin gives of the library founded in York by Archbishop Albert, in the eighth century, has been so frequently quoted, that I will not repeat it, but content myself with observing, that though it begins with a profession that it contained "all that the Roman world had produced, all that Greece had transmitted to Latium, all the celestial streams of which the Hebrew people had drunk," when he descends to particulars we hear of Jerome and Hilary, Ambrose and Augustine, Athanasius, Orosius, St. Gregory, and Pope Leo: and it is only after a long enumeration that he comes to the

[1] Quoted in Taylor's Transmission of Ancient Books to Modern times.

> "Historici veteres Pompeius, Plinius, ipse
> Aristoteles acer, rhetor quoque Tullius ingens."

Then comes again a long list of the Latin Christian poets,[1] while a single line is given to

> "Maro Virgilius, Statius, Lucanus et auctor
> Artis Grammaticæ."

I must express my doubts, whether the library contained any Hebrew MSS., or any Greek classic, and whether the Aristotle spoken of was not the Latin translation of a part of his works, made by Boethius. *Pompeius*, too, can hardly have been Trogus Pompeius, the historian of the world, in forty-four books, but the abridgment by Justin, which we still have. Horace, Virgil, Sallust, and Statius, are mentioned as being studied and copied at Paderborn, in North Germany, where a school and convent had been established by Charlemagne. The Abbat of Hildesheim, another of these establishments, is recorded to have got together a library consisting both of sacred and philosophical books. But north of the Alps Greek books appear to have been exceedingly rare. One practice of the monks, both of the East and West, was very injurious to literature.[2] The dearness of parchment led them, especially in the eleventh and twelfth centuries, to efface the original writing of a MS., and to write over it the life of a saint or a work of one of the Fathers. Such MSS. are called *palimpsests*. A remarkable instance is that of a Paris MS., where

---

[1] Among these *Alcuinus* has intruded himself, against the sense and the metre, into the place of *Alcimus* in Gale X Script., 1, 730.

[2] Robertson, Charles V., Illustration 477.

a very ancient copy of the New Testament has been effaced, to be supplied by a work of Ephrem the Syrian. Of these palimpsests we shall have to speak again, under the head of the Recovery of the Classics.

In the thirteenth century the East and the West of Europe were in a strongly contrasted state. Both had suffered from the enervating effects of the despotic sway of Rome; but the West had been renovated by the infusion of Teutonic and Scandinavian blood; and after struggling through a long period of confusion and darkness, had attained to settled forms of government, in which the spirit of political freedom was working, though as yet with partial and irregular efforts. Learning had never been extinct, but it had been monopolized by ecclesiastics, and philosophy had fallen under the exclusive domain of Aristotle. The Eastern Empire, no doubt, thought itself fortunate in having escaped from conquest; but its protracted life was only a long disease, ending in a state of mental imbecility. Yet it was reserved by Divine Providence to be the instrument of a mighty change,—to emancipate the mind of the West,—to introduce a purer taste, a spirit of freer thought in religion and philosophy, —to turn science from idle subtleties to the investigation of the great Laws of the Universe. In the literature of Greece the East preserved a precious seed. It was indeed like the seed enclosed in the swathings of a mummy; it was useless, for it had neither air, nor light, nor moisture, nor soil. But in the West a congenial soil was awaiting it. How it was transmitted to this soil, how it germinated and grew there, what harvests it has produced and yet promises to produce, will be subjects of our inquiry in the following Lecture.

V.

THE RECOVERY OF CLASSICAL LITERATURE.

We have reached the time when the history of Classical Literature was transferred from Eastern to Western Europe. We must, however, return a little upon our steps, to see what had been taking place here in the period immediately preceding the Capture of Constantinople.

There never was a time when the Latin classics were wholly neglected in the West, though, as we have seen,[1] the Christian Fathers held the first place in the mediæval libraries, and the Christian poets the second. The Abbey and School of Fulda, in Hesse Cassel, was one of the oldest ecclesiastical establishments in North Germany, having been founded by Bonifacius, the Apostle of Germany, in the eighth century, and endowed by Charlemagne, whose leading motive in establishing monasteries was to multiply schools, in which youths might be trained in learning and virtue.[2] In the ninth century it enjoyed a high celebrity, being presided over by Rabanus Maurus, a pupil of Alcuin, and a

---

[1] Page 154.   [2] Hospinian de Scholis, p. 94.

man accomplished in every branch of the learning of that age. To Fulda pupils resorted, not only from Germany, but from France, and among them was Lupus, who no doubt imbibed from Rabanus, himself one of the best Latin writers of the Middle Ages, that taste for Latin literature, which induced him, when he became Abbat of Ferriéres, to enrich his convent-library with copies of the classics. Twelve monks were regularly employed in transcription. There is a large collection of his letters extant, which are not only a proof of his own learning, but show what pains he took to make his classical library complete. One of them is addressed to Pope Benedict III., in which he requests his Holiness to send him copies of Quintilian, of Donatus on Terence, of Sallust, and several of Cicero's works which were not to be obtained in France.[1] We must not omit to mention, that in another letter he makes application for the loan of Quintilian, and a work of St. Jerome, from the Library of York. Paderborn and Hildesheim were hardly inferior to Fulda in the activity with which learning was cultivated, and books, including the Latin classics, collected or transcribed. In the schools of the Benedictines there are said to have been men learned in Hebrew, Greek, and Arabic.[2] These efforts for the improvement of libraries and the encouragement of learning were counteracted in England, as well as in northern France and Germany, by the ravages of the Danes and Northmen. It was not, however, by pagan and barbarous invaders that the Library of York was

[1] Heeren, I, 139.   [2] Hosp. de Schol., u. s.

destroyed, but by the Christian and civilized Normans, when the city was set on fire in the northern insurrection.

Another eminent churchman to whom literature is indebted for exertions to complete and multiply copies of the classics is Gerbert, afterwards Sylvester II., who became Pope in the last year of the tenth century. He was a man of varied talents and astonishing attainments, and has left a name even more remarkable in the history of science than that of literature. His knowledge of astronomy and mathematics, which was so great as to cause him to be taken for a magician, he is said to have learnt from the Arabs in Spain. From his letters he appears not only to have been familiarly acquainted with Sallust and Cæsar, Suetonius and Cicero, but to have spared no expence in collecting MSS. and procuring transcripts. He read the Republic of Cicero,[1] so long lost to us, and of which even now we possess only fragments. He had travelled widely, and had friends and correspondents in various parts of Europe, whom he employed in furtherance of his literary projects. The system of the Church was a bond of union among the remotest parts of European Christendom; the convents especially kept up a friendly intercourse with each other, which greatly facilitated the interchange of MSS. Italy was naturally much richer in these than France or Germany. In a letter to the Abbat of Tours, to whom he sends a list of the books which he desired to have copied, he writes,

---

[1] "Comitantur iter tuum Tulliana opuscula et De Republica et in Verrem." Ep. 87, ad Constantinum.

"You know how intent I am on the formation of a library. As I have in past times obtained, at great cost, from Rome and other parts of Italy, from Germany and Belgium, copies of books, being aided by the kindness of my friends, so now allow me to implore the same service from you. The expence of parchment, and what else is necessary, I will thankfully repay to your order." The interchange of books, however, was not always safe for the lender. Gerbert writes to the monks of an Italian convent, "You keep some books which rightfully belong to our Church, against the laws of God and man. If you return them our charity shall return to you with increase; the unjust detention of the deposit shall be repaid by the punishment you deserve." The example of Sylvester II. does not appear to have been followed by his successors in the eleventh century, who were more intent on establishing the independence of the spiritual power, than in promoting the cause of literature. A great decline in monastic discipline and learning took place in the century which followed his death, which gave rise to the proverb, "Monacho indoctior."[1] Yet bright streaks began to appear in this century, which shewed the approach of a fuller light. Among these may be reckoned the establishment of a school of law at Bologna, and a school of medicine at Salerno. Jurisprudence and medicine are essentially learned professions. The Civil Law, as taught at Bologna, was derived from ancient Rome. In countries where the Civil Law prevails, as in Holland, some eminent critics have been jurisconsults by profession.

[1] Hospinian, u. s.

The new study of the scholastic philosophy in the eleventh century, which began with Anselm and Lanfranc at Bec in Normandy, indicates an increased knowledge of Aristotle's writings, probably not derived directly from the Greek. The immediate effects of this study, which was made popular, and established in the Universities, by the Mendicant Friars, were not favourable to classical studies. The style of Aquinas, Scotus, and other Doctors of this school of subtilties, when compared with the Latinity of Lupus and Sylvester, is harsh and rude, and their nomenclature barbarous. But the scholastic philosophy had a most important influence on the progress of free thought. Its object was to combine logic, metaphysics, and theology, into an harmonious system, and the very attempt to do so was an acknowledgment, that reason had a claim to be heard, in matters hitherto decided by Church authority. Granting that their speculations were unpractical and fanciful, the schoolmen are not to be summarily dismissed, as vain and frivolous disputers. The want of the age, the necessary preliminary of all succeeding progress, was to set the minds of men in motion, and this the schoolmen effectually did. If they and their disciples sometimes fought with shadows, they at least kept themselves in salutary activity by this exercise, and prevented the faculties from becoming paralyzed by disuse. The very same order of men who, in their capacity of Mendicant Friars, were a chief means of riveting the chains of ecclesiastical authority, as teachers of the scholastic philosophy, prepared the means of breaking them. The state of neglect in which the MSS. of the classics were found in the monasteries, when research for them was set on foot, at a subsequent period has been ascribed with probability to the predominant taste for the scholastic philosophy, and the almost exclusive value set on Aristotle's writings, which were read in translations. Paris, Oxford, and Cambridge, were the chief seats of this system of instruction. We find traces, however, in the thirteenth century, of an increased acquaintance with the Greek language, the fruit, no doubt, of the Crusades, and of intercourse with the East. Roger Bacon and Michael Scot both appear to have read Aristotle in the original.

"In the resurrection of learning," says Gibbon, "Italy was the first that cast away her shroud." The long struggle between the Guelphs and the Ghibellines, the partizans respectively of the papal and the imperial power, had led to the emancipation of the principal towns of Tuscany from the power of their Dukes. Pisa, Lucca, Siena, and Florence, had made themselves independent republics. Florence soon distinguished itself above the rest, by the extent of its commerce, the freedom of its constitution, its literary culture, and its eminence in art. The same result, as regards political independence and commercial wealth and activity, had been attained in Northern Italy, though not as regards literature and art, which fixed their home in Florence.

Of the three great founders of Italian literature, Dante appears to have had no extraordinary attainments in classical scholarship. He understood no

Greek, and though he makes Virgil his guide through the infernal regions, he manifests no great familiarity with his works, or those of the other Latin poets. Perhaps this independence of foreign or extraneous aid may be one reason, why he still towers by force of native genius above his countrymen, who in their day enjoyed a much larger share of popularity. It was otherwise with Petrarch. Being endowed by nature with the finest taste for whatever was beautiful and great, he attached himself enthusiastically, from his earliest years, to the study of the classics, and especially of Cicero.[1] He found some of his writings among his father's books, who was a Florentine lawyer. Young Petrarch was one of those

> "Clerks foredoomed their father's soul to cross,
> Who pen a stanza when they should engross;"

and the relation between them was much the same as between Sir Walter Scott and his father, so pleasantly shadowed out in the two Fairfords in Redgauntlet. It was the father's ambition to see his son in doctorial robes, such robes, we may suppose, as Portia wears, when she comes, as the deputy of old Bellario of Padua, to rescue Antonio from the knife of Shylock. Coming one day suddenly upon him, and finding him reading, not the Pandects or the Digest, but Cicero and Virgil, he flung them into the fire, and they were half burnt before he was prevailed upon, by his son's earnest supplications, to restore them. He had the good sense, however, not further to thwart his son's inclinations. He

---

[1] Tiraboschi, 5, 415.

abandoned the legal profession, and declined that of the Church, that he might devote himself to letters.

Though Petrarch's fame now rests on his Italian poetry, his writings in the Latin language are far more numerous, and it was by his "Africa," a Latin epic on the Second Punic War, of which Scipio is the hero, that he hoped to gain immortality. We have to speak of him for his lifelong exertions to recover and preserve copies of the Latin classics. This object he never lost sight of, wherever he went and however he was engaged. "When my friends," says he, "were taking leave of me, and asked me, as friends do, 'Whether they should bring me anything on their return,' I used to answer, 'Nothing but the works of Cicero.' And how often did I send entreaties and money, not only throughout Italy, where I was pretty well known, but through Gaul and Germany, and even to Spain and Britain, —nay, strange to say, even into Greece, whence, though I expected Cicero, I got Homer. Whenever I went on a distant journey, if I happened to espy an ancient monastery from a distance, I straitway turned aside thither; 'For who knows,' said I, 'whether I may not find here some of the things of which I am in search.' When I was twenty-five years old, on a hasty journey between Holland and Switzerland, on my arrival at Liège, hearing that there was good store of books there, I stopped and detained my companions, till I could copy an oration of Cicero with my own hands, and a friend another. You will smile to hear that in a barbarian city, [everything North of the Alps was barbarous to the Italians,] of such goodly size, we had some difficulty in finding a little ink, and that, too, of the colour of saffron." Petrarch mentions Britain in this extract, as one of the countries from which he endeavoured to obtain MSS. Next to Cicero, Livy was the object of Petrarch's research. From the great bulk of his History, consisting of 140 books, it was generally transcribed in decads in the Middle Ages, and of these he possessed the first, third, and fourth. He sought for the second with great assiduity, but it was nowhere to be found, nor has it yet been recovered.

It is evident that the age in which Petrarch lived was a very critical one for classical literature. Had such a zealous collector arisen fifty years earlier, much might have been saved which is irretrievably lost: had the task been delayed another half century, our losses would have been still greater. It was known to Petrarch, that Cicero's Treatise de Republica had been extant in the Middle Ages, and he long entertained the hope of recovering it, but was at length convinced that it had disappeared.[1] He had himself a copy of Cicero's De Gloria, which he lent to his old master, who lived at Avignon, where Petrarch resided for many years. This man pledged the MS., and it has never since been heard of. Petrarch had read in his youth a treatise of Varro, "Libri Rerum Divinarum et Humanarum;" when he sought for a copy of it later in life, it was nowhere to be found, nor has it ever re-appeared. It is mortifying to reflect, that these precious remains of antiquity,

[1] Ep. fam., 7, 4.

after having passed through the perils of nine centuries, should have been lost only 100 years before the invention of printing.

The friend and younger contemporary of Petrarch, Boccacio, is best known as the first author of classic prose style in Italy, but he rendered good service to ancient literature, by the collection of Greek and Latin authors, especially the former.[1] The Greek language had never become wholly extinct in that part of Italy, which, from the number of its Dorian and Ionian colonies, had obtained the name of Magna Græcia. Boccacio brought from Calabria to Florence, Leo Pilatus, the first public teacher of the Greek language in Italy, and maintained him at his own expence. Neither Boccacio nor Petrarch appear to have advanced so far as to read Homer in the original, but Boccacio, by the help of Leo, composed a prose Latin version of both the Iliad and the Odyssey. At his death he bequeathed his library of Greek and Latin books to a convent in Florence. To form such collections became a fashion. Petrarch complains, that some bought books, as others pictures or furniture, for show and not for use, and some in order to sell them again at a higher price. No doubt it was a grievance to poor scholars, that the price of books should be raised, but we know, in the case of antiquities, that the surest incentive to their research and preservation is, the knowledge that there is a good market for them. There was no danger that MSS. of the classics should be used to light fires, when it was known that book collectors and booksellers were

[1] Ginguené, Hist. Lit. d'Italie, 3, 13.

ready to pay a good price for them. The negotiations respecting a reconciliation between the Eastern and Western Churches, which the impending danger of the Eastern produced, brought some eminent Greeks to Italy, one of whom, Manuel Chrysoloras, remained there as professor of Greek at Florence. His lecture rooms were crowded with hearers, to whom he explained the principles of the Greek language, and taught the Greek authors, Homer again leading the way in this resurrection of Greek literature, as he had presided over its birth in his native land.[1]

Before the commencement of the fifteenth century Greek was generally taught in all the universities of Italy, and the scarcity of Greek books (for we are still more than half a century from the introduction of printing into that country,) caused MSS. to be eagerly sought after, in lands where the Greek language was or had been spoken. The celebrated Francis Filelfo, who had been secretary to the Venetian embassy at Constantinople, and afterwards in the service of the emperor John Palæologus, has given a list of the Greek authors whom he had collected; they amount to upwards of fifty, and among them are the most illustrious names in Greek literature,—Homer, Pindar, Herodotus, Thucydides, Euripides, Aristotle, Plato, Demosthenes. He appears to have impoverished himself by the expenditure of large sums in these purchases, but he found munificent patrons in the great men of that age,—Cosmo de Medici,

[1] See in Gibbon, ch. 66, the enthusiastic description of his own feelings, given by one of the pupils of Chrysoloras.

Visconti, duke of Milan, Popes Nicolas V. and Pius II.; and various universities contended for the possession of him as a professor. His restless temper made his life a series of quarrels and changes, and the bitterness of his satire exposed him more than once to the danger of assassination.

With the name of Filelfo is naturally connected that of Poggio Bracciolini,[1] as equally ardent in the recovery of MSS. of the classics, though they were bitter enemies, and poured out on each other torrents of the vilest abuse. The circumstances of his life led him chiefly to the repositories of Latin MSS. Like Petrarch, he was the son of a lawyer, and having received a classical education under Manuel Chrysoloras, attracted by his talents the notice of Boniface IX., who appointed him his secretary for apostolic letters, and he remained attached to the papal court, through many successive popedoms. The Council of Constance, held in 1414, gave him an opportunity of examining the library of the Monastery of St. Gal, which is a few leagues distant, and he was rewarded by the discovery of a perfect copy of the Institutions of Quintilian, and a considerable part of the Argonautica of Valerius Flaccus. These precious remains, he tells us, he found buried in rubbish and dust, grievously mutilated, and lying in heaps on the lowest floor of a tower, not fit even to be a prison, in a room without door or window. In several other instances, as in the discovery of a copy of Cicero's oration for Cæcina, in a Cluniac monastery at Langres, and of

---

[1] Shepherd's Life of Poggio Bracciolini, Tiraboschi, vol. 6, p. 282, seq. for the life and writings of Filelfo.

Frontinus de Aquæductibus, in that of Monte Cassino, the MSS. appear to have been entirely neglected, and their value to have been unknown to their possessors; so that the time was fully come, for the monks to yield their trust to more vigilant and more intelligent guardians. Of the state of learning among the German monks we have an unexceptionable testimony from Trithemius, the learned Abbat of Spanheim, a Benedictine, and himself one of the greatest scholars of the age. "This time [he is speaking of the fourteenth century] was one in which the monks had entirely abandoned all literary study, and the observance of regular discipline was at an end."[1]

Poggio's duties called him to a great variety of places, and he made special journeys for the purpose of discovering copies of the classics. We have been so long in possession of them, that we can hardly understand the enthusiasm with which each new discovery was hailed. A friend of Poggio writes to him,—" As Camillus, on account of his having rebuilt Rome, was called its second founder, so you may be denominated the second author of all those pieces, which are restored to the world by your meritorious exertions. I therefore most earnestly entreat you, not to relax in your laudable designs. Let not the expense discourage you: I will take care to provide the necessary funds. We have now the entire treatise of Quintilian, of which before we had only one-half, and that in a very mutilated condition. O what a valuable acquisition! what an unexpected pleasure! Shall I then behold

[1] Chronic. Hirsaug. ad ann. 1300.

Quintilian whole and entire, who, even in an imperfect state, was a source of delight? I entreat you, my dear Poggio, send me the MS. as soon as possible, that I may see him before I dye. When after having delivered him from his long imprisonment in the dungeons of the barbarians, you transmit him to this country, all the nations of Italy ought to assemble to bid him welcome." Burmann says, Poggio obtained the MS. from the library of St. Gal "*honesto furto.*"[1] Where it now is appears uncertain, but the great majority of the MSS. of Quintilian are transcripts from it, made between this time and the invention of printing. The joy of Poggio's friend at the prospect of reading it was not excessive. No ancient author displays more correct taste, more just morality, and sounder notions of practical education than Quintilian, and the publication of his Institutes contributed greatly to the improvement of style. It is to be regretted that, belonging to the silver age of Latinity, he has been almost banished from the modern course of classical reading.

Besides Quintilian, many other authors, or portions of authors, were recovered by Poggio. Cardinal Beaufort invited him to England, and, after keeping him long in suspense, bestowed on him, though a layman, a small ecclesiastical benefice, —an abuse not uncommon in the Middle Ages. Its amount was not sufficient to retain him in a country so uncongenial to an Italian's feelings. We hear of no classical discoveries or researches made during his residence here.

[1] Praefatio ad Quintiliani Instit.

Filelfo and Poggio had not hesitated to impoverish themselves by their collection of MSS.; the wealth of the House of Medici enabled them to render the same service to letters, on a much ampler scale.[1] Cosmo, who for thirty years from 1434 was at the head of the Republic of Florence, was an ardent admirer of the Platonic philosophy, which is recommended to men of taste, by those charms of style, which are so entirely wanting in Aristotle. From the scholars, who formed a kind of Platonic Academy around him, he had imbibed an ardent passion for Greek literature. The foreign agents, who were established for commercial purposes in all the principal cities, had unlimited power to purchase Greek books; he kept a number of skilful copyists at work, and sent out learned men expressly for the purpose of examining monastic libraries. Aurispa, whom he sent into the East, returned with not fewer than 238 Greek MSS. Their acquisition was facilitated by the distracted state of the Eastern empire, and the dread of the Turks. In such circumstances books are the objects which their possessors most readily agree to part with. His grandson Lorenzo followed in his steps, and being disengaged from commercial pursuits, and less harassed by faction than his grandfather, he was able to devote himself entirely to art and literature. To enlarge and improve the Medicean library founded by Cosmo was an object of almost passionate earnestness with him, and he declared himself ready and even desirous, to prove his devotion to this object, by pledging his household furniture, if

---

[1] Roscoe, Lorenzo de' Medici, 1, 37, 2, 60.

necessary. Angelo Poliziano, one of the most tasteful of Italian scholars, had the charge of the library. By the close of the fifteenth century there remained only a gleaning to reward research after classical authors. Lorenzo sent emissaries to Greece to purchase MSS. there, especially from the monasteries on Mount Athos, which was covered with them from top to bottom. Janus Lascaris was returning with 200 Greek MSS., and in his last hours Lorenzo expressed to his friends, Pico of Mirandola and Poliziano, his earnest desire, that he might live long enough to behold them. It was not books alone that Lorenzo collected; the works of ancient art, which form the treasure of the Florentine Museum, and which, besides their intrinsic beauty, have afforded valuable materials to critics for the illustration of ancient authors,—the medals, vases, statues, and bas-reliefs,—were chiefly brought together by him.

Hitherto we have heard little of libraries at Rome, but in the year 1447 Tommaso Sarzano ascended the papal throne, under the title of Nicolas V. His attainments were of an extraordinary kind, no branch of science or letters, sacred or profane, was strange to him; and according to a contemporary, if you heard him speak on any one, you would suppose he had made that his sole study.[1] It appears to have been his object to make the library of the Vatican, which had been hitherto of small account, a complete repository of

---

[1] His life has been written at great length by Georgi. Rome, 1742. There is also a very interesting memoir of him by a contemporary in Muratori Script. Rer. It., vol. 25.

all the Greek and Latin writers. The capture of Constantinople, which took place during his papacy, afforded him great facilities for enlarging his collections. He kept a staff of skilful copyists, whom he established in different places, where there were books to be transcribed.[1] Though he lived only eight years after his election, he had accomplished so much, that the Vatican became the richest in MSS. of all the European libraries. Unfortunately it is also the least accessible, and therefore the least known and used.

We have now arrived at the epoch of the discovery of printing, which has placed literature beyond the reach of those vicissitudes which we have been describing. By the middle of the fifteenth century, type printing, due probably to Lawrence Costar of Harlem, had been so far improved by Gutenberg, Fust, and Schaeffer, that only minor changes remained to be made. It was no accident that connected the invention of printing with the revival of letters and the increased desire of reading. The new demand, as in other cases, set men's wits to work to devise the means of supply, and from the art of block printing, long known in the East, by various but rapid steps, typography was developed. It was speedily applied in Italy to the classics. In 1472, Virgil was printed at Florence; and Homer in 1488: before the end of the century 300 books had issued from the Florentine press. The work was carried on by the Juntas, the Aldi, and the Stephens, and before the end of the sixteenth

[2] Tiraboschi, 6, p. 1, p. 56, seq. 125.

century all the classical authors had been repeatedly printed.

Since the sixteenth century little has been added to the catalogue of the classics. The discovery of an Homeric Hymn (if it be Homer's), made by Matthäi at Moscow, is an exception, and there may be others, but they are of very trifling amount. Often have scholars flattered themselves, that from the Imperial library at Constantinople, or a monastery in Sicily, or a convent in Greece, the missing books of Polybius or Diodorus, or the lost decads of Livy, were about to be produced; but these hopes have proved fallacious. It might seem as if Europe had been so thoroughly ransacked, that there is hardly a corner where it is possible that a classic should be lying hid. But let us not abandon hope. When the Hellenic nation resumes its ancient patrimony, and a Christian sovereign occupies the palace of the Turk, is it improbable that they may find in some of its chambers, a portion of the literary treasures of their forefathers, which has been lying there for centuries, unheeded by its barbarous possessors?

It was natural that when the buried cities of the South of Italy, Herculaneum and Pompeii, were discovered in the last century, high hopes should be entertained of valuable additions to classical literature. Nor have these hopes been wholly fallacious. In Herculaneum there was found a number of rolls of papyrus, partially charred by the hot volcanic mud which overwhelmed the town, but still legible, and capable by care and management of being unrolled and transcribed. This has been done, but their contents have not proved of much value.[1] They consist almost entirely of the works of Philodemus, a contemporary of Cicero, and apparently of some local celebrity in the South of Italy, who was an admirer of Epicurus, and had collected his works. One Latin work only was found among the rolls—a poem on the Battle of Actium. In Pompeii, which has furnished such an ample and curious collection to the Museum of Naples, not a single volume has yet been found, the shower of hot ashes which buried the town having perhaps consumed them; or as very little money has been found, and as it is evident that after the eruption the inhabitants dug down into their houses, they may have carried off their books.

A real accession to the recovered works of the classics has been made by the reading of what are called *palimpsest* MSS., of which I spoke in my former Lecture. The practice of using writing materials twice over is certainly as old as the time of Cicero, who says in a letter to Trebatius, a lawyer, "I praise your economy in writing on a palimpsest, though I am curious to know what it was that you thought of so little value, that you effaced it in order to write me this letter. Perhaps it was some of your own law papers." This, however, was a palimpsest of papyrus; of course the more costly material of parchment would be used with similar economy. It was washed and then smoothed with pumice stone. This practice prevailed

---

[1] See Hayter on Herculaneum MSS. The process of unrolling and transcribing was still going on when I was at Naples in 1840, but nothing of importance has been discovered.

extensively in the Middle Ages.¹ Fortunately the process of expunging was not so complete, but that the original characters could be traced by care, and thus valuable fragments of the ancient classics, and later Latin authors, have been discovered. The glory of these discoveries belongs almost exclusively to one man, Angelo Mai, who before his death became head librarian of the Vatican, and had a Cardinal's hat. The Ambrosian library at Milan contained many MSS. which had been brought from the ancient Monastery of Bobio, founded by Columbanus in 642. They had probably been placed there by Gerbert, of whom we have already spoken as a zealous collector of MSS. Mai has related in his preface to the edition of the fragments of Cicero's Oration for Scaurus, how this discovery flashed upon him. He was examining a MS. of Sedulius, a Christian poet of the fifth century, one of those whom Alcuin mentions in his lines on Archbishop Albert's library, when he discovered traces of a former writing underneath. Joy almost surprised the abbat out of his professional proprieties. "O Deus immortalis, I suddenly exclaimed, what is it I see? Behold Cicero, the light of Roman eloquence, buried in undeserved darkness. I recognise the lost orations of Tully." Soon after he discovered considerable remains of the Epistles of Fronto, a correspondent of both the Antonines and of Lucius Verus.² But his crowning labour was the detection, among the

---

¹ See p. 154. Palimpsests of papyrus are in existence. See Mai Præf. ad Cic. Repub., p. 31.

² Reprinted by Niebuhr with his own notes and those of Buttmann and Heindorf, Berlin, 1816.

palimpsests of the Vatican, of Cicero's Treatise de Republica, hidden under a commentary by St. Augustine. This is the work which Petrarch had sought without success, but which had been lost to the world since the 12th century, except the Dream of Scipio, which had been preserved in a detached form. Though after all only a fragment of the work, in which Cicero described the constitution of his country, almost at the moment when it was about to fall a victim to the ambition of Cæsar and its own corruption, its recovery was most welcome to scholars. Niebuhr was enabled by it to form a more exact conception of the Servian Constitution, than he had been able to attain from other sources.[1] Mai has collected fragments of numerous other Greek and Latin authors from palimpsests, which he has published in several 4to volumes. Here then we close the history of the Recovery of Classical Literature, leaving however a blank page for future additions, of which I by no means despair.

As the account now stands, what have we lost, what have we saved? The first muster after a battle or a wreck is a melancholy sight. Many a brave fellow has been buried in the waves, or laid beneath the turf; the survivors, with scarred and mutilated limbs, exhibit a ghastly spectacle. The first impression, however, usually goes beyond the the actual loss; stragglers come dropping in; wounds which seemed mortal are healed by skilful surgery. If gashes still remain, use reconciles us to the sight of them, and from these diminished

---

[1] Roman History.—"The Centuries," 1, 373. Eng. Tr.

numbers, a band effective for service may still be gathered. And so it is when we compare what has been lost with what has been preserved of the Greek and Roman classics. Quintilian, in the first chapter of his tenth Book, points out the best authors of either literature, and the comparison of his list with what is in our possession will give us an exact measure of our loss. We shall perhaps be surprised to find how little, of first rate excellence, has perished. We have the two immortal works of Homer, and about as much of Hesiod as we could desire. We can bear the loss of the whole race of Cyclic poets, since so much of their mythological history has been preserved to us in prose, and as poets they did not stand high. "Antimachus," says Quintilian, "is reckoned by the critics to come next after Homer;" but as he adds the remark, "that there was a long distance between the second and the first," "aliud *proximum* esse, aliud *secundum*," we may the less regret that his works have been lost. Among the lyric poets, we have only fragments of Alcæus and Sappho, Bacchylides and Corinna; but of Pindar, whom Quintilian pronounces to be "decem lyricorum facile princeps," the Coryphæus of the band of lyrists, we have four books of odes, no doubt those in which his genius was most fully displayed, as they celebrated the victors in the Grecian games. The havoc in dramatic literature has been great; seven tragedies alone remain of ninety which Æschylus wrote; seven only of the still more numerous works of Sophocles; but we have probably their masterpieces; and among the nineteen plays of Euripides there are several of inferior merit. In the Old Comedy, again, Aristophanes, whom we have, was considered by the ancients themselves as superior to Eupolis and Cratinus, whom we have not. The loss of Menander, Philemon, Diphilus, and the other writers of the New Comedy, is almost a solitary instance of the destruction of a whole class in literature, inadequately represented by their Latin translators and imitators; for Terence, as Julius Cæsar's epigram tells us, was but a *dimidiatus Menander*, wanting the comic power of his original. Herodotus, Thucydides, Xenophon, had no rivals in history among those who have been lost. In philosophy we have ample remains of Plato and Aristotle, the two great heads of opposite schools; the works of the Academics, the Epicureans, and the Stoics, have perished, with the exception of Epictetus; but none of them were remarkable for style, and we have other means of ascertaining what their doctrines were.

The Latin tragedies were translations or imitations of the Greek, so that the entire loss of the oldest specimens is only to be regretted in reference to the history of the language. In poetry the Romans could boast of no greater names than Lucretius, Catullus, Tibullus, Propertius, Virgil, Horace, and Ovid; in history, than Sallust, Cæsar, Livy, and Tacitus; and all these are in our classical library. We could greatly have desired an oration or two of Quintus Hortensius, but of his great rival, Cicero, we have such ample specimens as may console us for the loss of several inferior orators— Messala and Cælius, Sulpicius and Trachalus.

Every one, according to his own tastes and studies, will fix on some author or class of authors, whom he would specially desire to have saved from the wreck. Wordsworth has said,—

> "O ye who reverently explore
> The wreck of Herculanean lore,
> What rapture, could ye seize
> Some Theban fragment, or unrol
> One precious tender-hearted scroll
> Of pure Simonides."

And if, from the nook of an unexplored library, or unexamined palimpsest, a critic could produce a poem of Simonides, at all approaching in purity and tenderness to the song of Danae to her child, so beautifully translated by L. C. J. Denman,[1] every man of taste would rejoice in the discovery. Professor De Morgan again, if he were consulted, might ask for the lost books of the Arithmetic of Diophantus. But the spring of truth and tenderness is in the heart of man, and gushes forth in poetry in every land and language. We have lost all save a fragment of Simonides; but we have Burns and Tennyson and Hemans and Longfellow. The truths of science and philosophy are not created by moralists or mathematicians; they are in the mind and conscience and the reflecting intellect; they may be temporarily, but never irretrievably, lost. An historical fact, on the contrary, once lost, is lost for ever. I may be allowed, therefore, to say, that the most serious injury which the world has suffered is in the department of ancient historical literature. Great has been the destruction in both languages. The predecessors of Herodotus

[1] See Bland's Collections from Greek Anthology.

exist only in a few fragments. The same fate has befallen the successors of Xenophon in Grecian history. The contemporary historians of Alexander's life and actions are wholly lost, and we depend for this most important period on the second-hand evidence of Arrian and Q. Curtius. Little has been spared of what the Greeks wrote to illustrate the countries which they called barbarous. We have not one of their works on Egypt, between Herodotus in the fifth century B. C., and Diodorus in that of Augustus. The history of Manetho, derived from ancient monuments, has been lost, except a few pages preserved in Eusebius and Josephus. The Persian history of Ctesias we know only by extracts in Photius; the Lydian history of Xanthus remains in yet more scanty fragments. The Phœnicians, from whom the western world derived their alphabet, have reaped little benefit from their invention; their native historians have entirely perished; the Greek writers of their history nearly so. Had we the work of Fabius Pictor, or the poetical annals of Ennius and Nævius, there would be an end of much uncertain hypothesis respecting the early ages of Rome. Had Livy and Polybius been entire, what a blaze of eloquence would the one have shed on the later times of the Republic; what a philosophic light would the other have thrown upon the history of the wars, which made Rome the mistress of the world! Tacitus perhaps never lived to write that history of Trajan, which he had reserved for his tranquil old age; but we have certainly lost ten books of his Annals, and all but a single year of his Histories. When I think, had these lost works been preserved, with what ease and security the historical inquirer would have walked, where he must now grope and stumble, I feel more than ever grateful for the invention of printing, which guards us from any similar loss of historical evidence.

Imperfect, however, as the recovery of classical literature has been, it has wrought a change in the condition of Europe, the effects of which will long continue; for they are expanding and progressive; nor have I any fear, that the practical tendencies of our age will cause the neglect of the two noble languages in which that literature is preserved. The result of practical talent is often the acquisition of competence, and even wealth, by those who have gone through the world without a tincture of classical education, and the hasty conclusion is drawn, that Greek and Latin are useless. But their own convictions are different, for we almost invariably find them earnestly procuring for their children the culture which has been denied to themselves.

Probably the form of classical instruction will change; in our own recollection it has changed; it has admitted more of logic into its grammar, more of philosophy into its etymology; it has confined itself less to words to the exclusion of things, and it has thus taken a higher place in the discipline of the mind. There is, however, in the great writers of Greece and Rome, so much that is admirable in thought and style, that whatever may be the oscillations and excentricities of taste, they can never become obsolete, but will serve as models to future generations, as they have done to the past.

VI.

THE REIGN OF TRAJAN ILLUSTRATED BY A MONUMENT FOUND IN YORK.

```
IMP· CAESAR
DIVI·NERVAE·FIL·NERVA
TRAIANVS·AVG·GERM·DAC
PONTIFEX·MAXIMVS·TR
POTESTATIS·XII·IMP·VI·F.C
PER·LEG·VIIII·HISP.
```

The inscribed Tablet found at the end of 1854, in King's Square, received, at the time of its discovery, from the Curator of Antiquities, the late Rev. C. Wellbeloved, a complete *antiquarian* elucidation; but it has occurred to me that some additional interest might be given to it by a more *historical* illustration. I exhibit a copy of it, as restored by him, marking the restorations by inclined capitals.

Although the reign of Trajan was not short, lasting from A. D. 98—117, and was one of the most important, the most happy, and the most glorious which the Roman people enjoyed under their Cæsars, we are very destitute of literary materials for its history. The Lives of the Cæsars by Suetonius end with Domitian. Tacitus had reserved the reigns of Nerva and Trajan as a copious and easy subject for his old age. "Si vita suppeditet," says he, in the first section of his Histories, "principatum divi Nervæ et imperium Trajani, uberiorem securioremque materiam senectuti seposui : rarâ temporum felicitate ubi sentire quæ velis, et quæ sentias dicere licet." These words may have been written in the reign of Hadrian, to which they were still applicable, though less so than to Trajan's, at whose death, in A. D. 117, Tacitus was fifty-seven years old. But whether he died before the arrival of that old age for which he had reserved the history of Trajan's reign, or was prevented by other circumstances from undertaking it, he appears never to have written it, and we have not to reckon the loss of this, as of so large a portion of the Annals, among the injuries which Latin Literature has suffered from the scythe of time. The Greek history of Dion Cassius might have supplied the deficiency, but, unfortunately, of this portion we have only the Epitome, or Excerpta of Xiphilinus. The Panegyric of Trajan, by Pliny the Younger, is declamatory and vague; the correspondence between him and the Emperor during his Bithynian Administration is very instructive; but it embraces only a short time, and is limited to local subjects. This scarcity of historical writings gives an increased value to the monuments of Trajan's reign, and they are fortunately numerous and splendid. The bridge over the Danube, which was the wonder of his contemporaries, no longer exists, except in the ruins of its piers; but the bridge of Alcantara, the harbour of Civita Vecchia, the triumphal arches of Ancona and Beneventum, and the Column at Rome, with numerous smaller monuments, inscriptions, and coins, attest his activity, especially in the erection of public works and the improvement of the means of communications. He has indeed been ridiculed for his fondness for seeing his own name inscribed on walls, and Constantine is said to have nicknamed him *parietaria* (wall-flower, or, more properly, pellitory,) from this circumstance.[1] The reproach comes with a bad grace from Constantine, who plundered Trajan's Arch at Rome, to adorn his own with its bas-reliefs;[2] and certainly antiquaries and historians have cause to rejoice, that he multiplied the memorials of himself in all parts of his empire. Till our inscription was discovered, it was not known that Britain was among the countries so honoured.

The first of his titles is GERMANICUS. This had been conferred upon him before he became Emperor; for it happened that on the day of his adoption, at the end of October A. D. 97, letters arrived from Germany, wreathed, as the Roman custom was, with laurel, announcing a victory in Pannonia. Trajan was at that time commander of the army in Germany, but, apparently, was not with the victorious troops, as he is said to have been at Colonia Agrippina (Cologne on the Rhine) when he was adopted by Nerva. Nerva himself took the title of Germanicus on this occasion, which he bears on some of the coins of his short reign,[3] and gave it to his adopted son. He is called Imperator for the sixth time, which title he first received, not,

---

[1] Aurelius Victor Epitome, 41, c. 11. Ammian. Marcellin., 27, 3, 7.
[2] Nardini, 363.
[3] Cohen, Nerva, 35, with Trib. Pot. II.

as was usual, by a spontaneous acclamation of the army on the field of battle, after a victory, but from Nerva, when he made him his associate in the empire. "Will it be believed," says Pliny, in the ninth section of his Panegyric, "that the son of a man of patrician and consular dignity, and of one who had gained a triumph, who was in command of a very brave, numerous, and devoted army, should have been made Imperator, and not by his army, and that the title of Germanicus should have been sent to him from Rome at the very time when he was commanding in Germany? Nihil magis a te subjecto animo factum est, quam quod *imperare* cepisti." The number which follows Imperator on coins and inscriptions is therefore not a note of the number of years that a Cæsar had reigned, but of the number of victories which had procured him this title. In the same way, as Trajan did not take the consulship every year, the number subjoined to Cos. is no evidence of the year of his reign. But the tribunate, being annually renewed, marks the regnal year. It was conferred on Trajan at the same, or nearly the same, time as the title Imperator. "Simul filius, simul Cæsar, mox imperator et consors tribunitiæ potestatis, et omnia pariter et statim factus est." (Plin., c. 8.)

Dacicus appears next in the list of Trajan's titles. It is true it is only in the restored part of the monument, and perhaps those who are not accustomed to the study of inscriptions may look on this as a mere conjecture. But its correctness admits of no doubt. The style and title of imperial and royal personages is a settled and formulary thing, and as we have coins and inscriptions in great number, in which the titles Germanicus and Dacicus follow each other,[1] and as the space and symmetry of the stone exactly correspond with the abbreviated form DAC., in which this epithet usually appears, and as the date is prior to the time when Trajan assumed the epithet of Parthicus, namely, his nineteenth Tribunate,[2] A. D. 116, we may safely assume *Dacicus* to be the missing title.

The country which the Romans called Dacia answered mainly to the modern Wallachia and Transsylvania, but stretched also into Moldavia and Bessarabia. The banks of the Danube have been, in all ages, the region in which civilization and barbarism have come into collision. Darius crossed that river to conquer the Scythians, whose invasion had laid waste Asia Minor and Syria; Alexander crossed it to punish the Getæ, the same people as the Dacians, or closely allied to them. In the days of Augustus they were a source of alarm to the Roman people; Virgil reckons it one of the happy features of the rustic's lot, that he gives himself no concern about the "conjurato descendens Dacus ab Istro."[3] They were at this time in the state in which a barbarous people of nomadic origin is most formidable to its neighbours; they had been settled long enough on the frontiers of a civilized people to have improved in the art of war, while they retained all their original fierceness and appetite for conquest. Under their King Decebalus they

---

[1] Orelli, 785, seq.
[2] Eckhel, Doctr. Numm. Vett.
[3] Georg., 2, 497.

had obtained such power, that Domitian had agreed to pay them a yearly tribute. Trajan, who had come to Rome from Germany the year after his adoption, remained there till A. D. 101, when he took the command of the army in Pannonia (the modern Austria), and, crossing the Theiss, marched into Transylvania, along the valley of the river Maros, defeated Decebalus, and compelled him to sue for peace. He returned to Rome, enjoyed a triumph, and assumed the title of Dacicus, which first appears on his coins in the year 103, *i. e.*, five years before the date of our inscription.[1] In the interval he had earned a still better claim to it. He had scarcely reached Rome from the Danube when Decebalus broke the treaty which he had unwillingly made. Trajan returned to the banks of the Danube, which he crossed a little below the remarkable pass and rapid called "The Iron Gate," and marching into the heart of Transylvania, defeated the Dacians so completely, that their king put himself to death in despair. Trajan enjoyed a second triumph, in the year 106, on his return from this campaign.

It is the events of these two wars which are represented in the sculptures of Trajan's column at Rome. This celebrated monument, the first example, I believe, of the employment of a detached column, of such magnitude, for the purpose of a memorial, is 116 ft. in height, composed of thirty-four blocks, and is covered, from the pedestal to the summit, with a series of bas-reliefs in marble, of a very pure style, and most instructive to the

[1] Eckhel, pt. 2, vol. 6, p. 460.

antiquary and the historian. They afforded a study for ancient costume and armour to Raffaelle and his pupils, Giulio Romano and Francesco Polidoro, and they are represented with great accuracy and minuteness by Fabretti in the engraving now exhibited. The good taste of employing a member of architecture evidently designed, as a column is, to be the support of an architrave, as a mere memorial pillar, may be doubted; the Egyptian Obelisk was a better device. It is impossible that a spectator can see with any distinctness beyond the lowest sculptures. I cannot go into any detail respecting the events recorded on the Trajan Column; they are explained in the marginal remarks of Fabretti. The pedestal bears the date of the seventeenth tribunate of Trajan, *i. e.*, the year 113, so that it was several years in finishing; which is not wonderful, considering the multitude of elaborate sculptures with which it is covered. We are naturally surprised to find, that the inscription on the base contains no reference to the apparent purpose of its erection. It is S. POP. ROM. IMP. CÆS. DIVI. NERVÆ. FILIO. TRAJANO. AUG. GERM. DAC. PONT. MAX. TRIB. POT. XVII. COS. VI. P. P. AD DECLARANDUM QUANTÆ ALTITUDINIS MONS ET LOCUS TANTIS OPERIBUS SIT EGESTUS; the *opera* here spoken of being the Forum of Trajan, with its Basilica, Temple, and other buildings. The base of the Quirinal Hill had been excavated to a depth equalling the heighth of the column, and as a measure of this, not to glorify the emperor, it professes to have been erected. It was originally surmounted by a bronze statue of Trajan. This having perished, Sixtus V., a great restorer of the monuments of Rome, replaced it by a similar statue of the chief of the apostles, who, as Eckhel observes, wonders much what HE can have to do with the tumult and slaughter of the Dacian War, and the rites and emblems of idolatry.

The twelfth tribunate of Trajan, including part of the years A. D. 108, 9, is the date of the sculpture or erection of the tablet found in King's Square. Its brevity is tantalizing, for it affords us no means of deciding what the work was, the execution of which it records. From its size and form,[1] however, it must have been intended to have been affixed to some building, and a building of considerable magnitude and solidity. The position in which it was found, just beside the line of the Roman wall of York, where the symmetrical form of the castrum would lead us to look for a gateway, in a site to which tradition has assigned an imperial palace,[2] all seem to point to one conclusion. The date of the erection of the Roman walls of York has hitherto been considered quite uncertain. Will this tablet help us to define it?

If we review the history of Roman conquest and settlement in Britain, we shall, I think, be convinced, that there is nothing improbable in the supposition of Eburacum having been a walled city in the reign of Trajan. The subjugation of the

---

[1] In its perfect state it must have been 3 ft. 9 in. long, by 3 ft. 4 in. deep. The largest letters are six inches long, and they are all beautifully cut.

[2] Christ Church, near King's Square, is called in ancient charters, "Ecclesia S. Trinitatis in curia regis." The court of the Saxon and Norman kings would probably be on the site of the Roman prætorium. Drake, Eboracum, p. 319; Wellbeloved, Eburacum, p. 63.

Brigantes by Agricola took place about A. D. 79—80, and that York was then established as a Roman station seems a necessary consequence of its important central position. This does not necessarily imply its being surrounded with walls; but we generally find, that wherever a permanent castrum was established, the building of a wall followed, if not immediately, yet at no long interval. Perhaps the progress of Agricola may be considered too rapid, and his conquests, which reached to the foot of the Grampians, too extensive, to allow of his devoting sufficient time to the fortification of the castra which he established; and York may have been at first surrounded only with ramparts of earth. The profound silence of historians respecting the affairs of Britain under Trajan, who became emperor fourteen years after the recall of Agricola by Domitian, has led to the supposition that this island was entirely neglected by him. Our inscription proves that this was not the case; for it is evident that some work worthy of commemoration on a tablet so large and beautiful was performed in York by his command, through the instrumentality of the Ninth Legion, which appears to have been stationed here from the time of Agricola's return. It had been engaged in his Caledonian campaign, and had suffered severely in a night attack.[1]

That the construction of the walls of York is as old as Trajan's reign, is rendered probable by the very exact correspondence between their structure

---

[1] Tacitus, Vit. Agric., c. 26. "Hostes universi nonam legionem, ut maxime invalidam, adgressi, inter somnum et trepidationem caesis vigilibus irrupere."

and a mode of building which we know to have prevailed at that time. Among the letters of Pliny to Trajan, contained in the tenth book, is one (48) relating to the theatre of Nicæa. The walls had huge cracks in them, and the building threatened to become a ruin. "The architect," says Pliny, "(it is very true he is a rival of the man who began the work) affirms that the walls, though they are 22 feet thick, are not adequate to support the weight laid upon them, 'quia sine cæmento medio farcti, nec testaceo opere præcincti;' because they are filled in without hewn stones in the middle, or having a band of brick work." Now if any one will examine the structure of the remarkable portion of the wall which is preserved in our grounds, he will see, that it is filled in with rubbish, like the wall of the theatre of Nicæa, the *cæmenta*, or squared stones, not going through the wall. But, unlike the Nicæan architect, the builder *has* strengthened his work by a band of brick, *opere testaceo præcinxit*.[1] This passage has been a source of perplexity to the commentators; one of them takes *cæmento* in the sense of mortar, which it never has in the classics, who always use it of hewn, squared stones; another supposes the *opus testaceum* to mean a composition of pounded brick and lime, *opus signinum*, which, however suitable for flooring or plaster, could not strengthen a wall, nor could its use be called *præcinctio*.

This mode of building with rows of bricks at

---

[1] Testa is more commonly used of paving tiles; but the bricks which form the præcinctio of Roman walls are generally thin, like tiles.

certain intervals is very general in the Roman remains in the South; it is seen at Richborough, at Pevensey, at Lymne, at Colchester, London, Verulam, Wroxeter, and generally where there are any remains of Roman walls; but nowhere, as far as I recollect, north of York, certainly not along the line of Hadrian's Wall, the remains of which are so considerable, nor in the few specimens of Roman masonry which remain in Scotland. The same structure prevailed in the portion of the wall between the Multangular Tower and Bootham Bar.[1] The correspondence between the architecture of our wall and Pliny's description does not indeed prove that they *were* built in Trajan's time; it only proves that they *may* have been. Nor, again, does the tablet say that the ninth legion built the wall of Eburacum; but we can hardly believe that a camp with a mere rampart of earth would be honoured by the erection of such a monument as ours. The Romans had received a warning, by the capture of Camalodunum, of the consequences of leaving their towns unwalled. Tacitus, speaking of it, says (Ann. 14, 31), it seemed easy to destroy the colony, "nullis munimentis septam," and accordingly it was destroyed, as were Londinium and Verulamium, then equally defenceless. The ninth legion was on that occasion the chief sufferer. It is probable, however, that, though walled at that time, Eburacum was merely a military station. We have never found within the area of Roman York traces of temples or costly dwelling-houses, such as the south side of the river has furnished. In this

[1] See plate 2 in Wellbeloved's Eburacum.

respect York is a remarkable contrast to Aldborough, where all the principal remains of antiquity are within the walls. York, we know, was made a colony; and it was probably after that event, and after the whole Brigantian region had been rendered secure by Hadrian's wall, that it became the abode of a considerable civil population, though without ceasing to be the chief military station of the north of Britain.

In no part of the present circuit of our walls has any monument been found, from which a precise date can be derived; but Mr. Wellbeloved, in his Eburacum, has given some inscriptions from the Multangular Tower, which contain the name of the Sixth Legion.[1] Now there is no reason to suppose that the Multangular Tower is of later erection than the rest of the walls; at least it appears to be of the same age as the part which adjoins it, since the courses run regularly through from one to the other. The Sixth Legion, we know, did not come to York till the reign of Hadrian, Trajan's successor.[2] Had there been anything in these inscriptions which indicated that the Sixth Legion had erected the Multangular Tower, we must have given up the claim for an earlier date. But they are not of this kind. Along the line of Hadrian's wall we find inscriptions, recording that such a Cohort of such a Legion built a certain length of it. The inscriptions in

---

[1] Ebur., p. 59, pl. 7.
[2] It came to York from Germany; Gruter, 457, 2, has a monument to M. Pontius, "Trib. Mil. Leg. VI. Vict. cum qua ex Germ. in Britan. transiit." See also Orelli, 3186.

the Multangular Tower convey no such intimation; they are mere scratchings on the stone, which may have been made long after its erection. They are in the lower apartment, which was apparently without any natural light. A soldier occupying it would find time nearly as heavy on his hands as a prisoner in the Tower, or in the dungeons of Venice. Under such circumstances a civilian relieves his tedium by handing down his name to posterity on the wall, to which a soldier naturally adds his regiment, or perhaps his commanding officer. The walls of the barracks at Pompeii exhibit such records. And to this I attribute the appearance of the name of L. ANTONIUS PRÆFECTUS MILITUM, and other military marks on the lower wall of the Multangular Tower. As far as we can judge from the forms of the characters, they are subsequent to the age of Hadrian.

So meagre are our accounts of the reign of Trajan, that we are almost entirely ignorant of the manner in which the years immediately succeeding his return from the second Dacian War were spent. Tillemont and others, misled by spurious coins and legends,[1] supposed him to have gone in the year 106 into the East, to have gained a victory over

---

[1] According to the Acts of the Martyrdom of Ignatius, (Cotelerius P. P. Apost. 2, 161,) Trajan came to Antioch in the ninth year of his reign (A. D. 106), being impressed with the belief, that unless he compelled the Christians, who had their chief quarter there, to sacrifice to idols, he should forfeit the favour of the gods, who had been so propitious to him in his Dacian war. He accordingly summoned the bishop Ignatius before his tribunal, and offered to make him *High Priest of Jupiter, and name him Father of the Senate*, if he would sacrifice to the gods. If the story had not been refuted by chronology, the absurdity of the dialogue would have shewn its true character.

the Parthians, and to have returned in 107 to Rome. But the more accurate investigations of Eckhel have shown, that no such Eastern expedition took place, and it is probable that this and the following year were spent in Rome. Some military operations of importance, however, must have been undertaken, if not by the Emperor, at least by his lieutenants; for while on our tablet he is called Imperator for the sixth time, he appears in the year 107 on the bridge of Alcantara[1] only as Imperator for the fifth time. It may have been given for the conquest of Arabia Petræa by Cornelius Palma.[2] We may conclude, therefore, that he was at Rome when he gave the command to execute the work, whatever it was, to which our tablet refers. No one who has read the tenth book of Pliny's Letters, and observed the minute attention which Trajan paid to all the affairs of Bithynia, will be surprised that he should have given directions respecting an erection at York. It was in this interval of peace that he improved the harbour of Ancona, and caused a road to be constructed through the Pontine Marshes, and from Beneventum to Brundusium, as well as in other parts of the empire. The Parthian War, under the emperor in person, appears not to have begun till 114, when Chosroes, king of Parthia, entered Armenia, and dispossessed the king, who was an ally of the Romans. He took the command of his armies, crossed the Euphrates into Mesopotamia, and, driving out the Parthians from several fortresses which they had occupied, was saluted PARTHICUS and IMPERATOR

---

[1] Gruter, 248, 1.   [2] Cohen, Trajan, no. 15, 309.

VII. by his army. The Parthians were, however, imperfectly subdued, and revolting in the year 116, Trajan deposed their king, and placed the diadem on the head of Parthamaspates. This event is recorded on a coin in our collection. Trajan never returned from this Eastern expedition. He died at Selinus in Cilicia in 117, and his ashes are said to have been brought to Rome and deposited at the base of his own column.[1]

The most honourable and interesting of the titles of Trajan is that of OPTIMUS PRINCEPS, or OP. alone, which does not appear either on our tablet or on his column, but which is found on some of the coins in our cabinet. It was early bestowed on him, as we may conclude from the words of Pliny, in his Panegyric, "adoptavit te optimus princeps in suum, senatus in *Optimi* nomen," (c. 88) and no Roman emperor had borne it before him, though it was an obvious compliment. "Paratum id quidem et in medio positum, novum tamen," says Pliny. It does not appear, however, to have been incorporated among his titles till some years later; according to the observation of the discriminating Eckhel, it first appears in coins of A.D. 103, and then on the reverse, and in the form S. P. Q. R. Optimo Principi. From the year 114 it is transferred to the obverse, and occupies the middle place between Trajanus and Augustus. Our cabinet contains examples of both. The epithet of PATER PATRIÆ, which the emperors ordinarily received with their other titles, and which was first bestowed on Julius Cæsar, Trajan declined till he had done

---

[1] Aur. Victor, c. 13.

something to deserve it. "Nomen illud quod alii primo principatûs die receperunt, Tu usque eo distulisti donec jam te mereri fatereris" (c. 21). It was not long deferred, as it is found on coins of A. D. 99, when he filled up again the thirty-five tribes of Rome, whose numbers had been much diminished, made five thousand new seats in the Circus, and distributed a *congiarium*, or largess of corn, wine, and oil, to the people. No emperor ever better deserved the title of Optimus than Trajan. Gibbon, after lamenting that we are reduced to collect his actions from the glimmerings of an abridgement, or the doubtful light of a Panegyric, observes, "There remains, however, one panegyric far removed beyond the suspicion of flattery. Above 250 years after the death of Trajan, the Senate, in pouring out the customary acclamations on the accession of a new emperor, wished that he might surpass the felicity of Augustus and the virtue of Trajan." He has received a testimony from a very different source. Gregory the Great, smitten with admiration of a humane act of Trajan, is said to have wept for his fate, as a heathen condemned to everlasting fire, till it was announced to him by revelation that he was liberated from the pains of hell, but on condition that Gregory should never presume to intercede for another infidel. I trust he has been delivered, whether by the intercession of St. Gregory, or not. There have been few Christian sovereigns who might not safely say, SIT ANIMA MEA CUM TRAJANO.

VII.

ON ROMAN WAXED TABLETS IN THE CURSIVE CHARACTER, FOUND IN TRANSYLVANIA.

The photographs which I now exhibit have been sent to me by my friend and former pupil, Mr. Paget, the author of a well-known work on Hungary, and now resident in Transylvania. They represent an almost unique class of documents, the history of which is very curious.

No educated person can need to be informed, that it was the custom of the Romans to employ thin tablets of wood, coated with wax, for memoranda, letters, drafts of agreements, first sketches of compositions and similar purposes. The school-boy, when he reads in Horace, "sæpe stylum vertas,"[1] is informed, that the Roman *stylus* was a metallic instrument, pointed at one end and broad at the other; that the pointed end was used for tracing characters on a waxed tablet, the broad end for smoothing the wax and effacing them. Consequently, to invert the style was to correct your composition. St. Jerome says of himself, alluding to the care with which he corrected his works, that he always preferred the end of the style which effaced to that which wrote.[2] Every collection of Roman antiquities contains specimens of the stylus, generally in bronze, sometimes in iron;[3] but till lately no example had been known

[1] Sat., 1, 10, 72.
[2] Epist., 51.
[3] Dextra tenet ferrum, vacuam tenet altera ceram. Ovid. Met. 9, 521, of Byblis preparing to write a letter.

of the waxed tablet on which the Romans wrote. Their use continued in the Middle Ages, when the papyrus had ceased to be a writing material, and linen paper had not been introduced. Charlemagne, according to the testimony of Eginhard,[1] used tablets in his abortive attempts to teach himself to write, and a mediæval German author, Notker, who lived at the end of the ninth century, describes himself as writing with a stylus *(griffel)* on a waxed tablet. A stylus has been found in many Frankish graves, (though never in Saxon [2]) but not accompanied with the tablets. Specimens of these, however, remain even of a late age. The public library of Geneva contains waxed tablets with the accounts of the steward of Philip le Bel, for the year 1308.[3] That they should not have been found in Herculaneum or Pompeii, buried in volcanic mud and ashes, is not surprising; but I am not aware that they have been discovered with other remains of Roman antiquity, under circumstances more favourable to their preservation. The mines of Transylvania have in an unexpected manner supplied the deficiency.

The conquest of Dacia by Trajan, as related in the preceding paper, was followed by Roman colonization.[4] It became a consular province, and was retained till the reign of Aurelian. It is rich in metals of every kind, except tin, and especially in gold.[5] The working of the gold mines was carried on in a very systematic manner, *Colleges, i. e.*

---

[1] Vit. Car. Magn., c. 25.
[2] Archæol., 37, 111.
[3] Sismondi, Hist. des Français, 6, 108. "Ces sont des tablettes, en bois enduites en cire."
[4] Eutropius, 6, 6.
[5] Paget, Hungary and Transylvania, vol. 1, ch. 12, 13.

incorporated companies, being established in several places. Of these gold mining establishments Abrudbánya in Transylvania appears to have been the chief, and to have borne the name of *Auraria*. At this day it is the principal mint of Transylvania, where the gold, collected in sand or nuggets from the streams, is coined, as well as what is obtained by more regular mining operations. The neighbourhood exhibits inscriptions and remains of the Roman times, and an arched entrance to a gold mine, of the solid construction which characterizes the works of that people.[1]

In a mine at Vöröspatak, not far from Abrudbánya, two pieces of a waxed tablet were discovered in 1786, on which letters could be traced, but by injudicious attempts at drying and rubbing they have been so much injured as to be now illegible.[2] A more important discovery of the same kind was made in the same district in 1788. In this case there were, it is said, five tablets; what became of two of them is unknown; three, which were on deal, came first into the hands of Paul Kovacs and afterward of Stephen Lazar, who deposited them in the library of the Unitarian College at Clausenburg, of which body he was Superintendent. Here they remained till 1811, when they were claimed by his son, and sold in 1834 by his grandson to a trading antiquary, who again sold them to an eminent collector in 1835, Nicolas Jancovich. By him

---

[1] Massmann, Libellus Aurarius, sive Tabulæ ceratæ. Lips., 1840, § 214, 215.

[2] Erdy, De Tabulis ceratis in Transsilvania repertis. Pest. 1856, p. 5. A communication to the Clausenburg Academy in 1861 by L. H. Finály Clausenb., 1861, treats of the same subject, in the Hungarian language.

they were sold to the National Museum of Hungary, at Pesth. In 1807 three tablets of beech wood are said by the trading antiquary before mentioned, to have been found in a mine at Toroczkö, and to have come into his hands. These, along with the three of deal before mentioned, were purchased by Jancovich and added to the National Museum. He had previously taken both sets with him to Munich, and submitted them to Dr. Massmann, Professor in the University of that city. Up to this time no one had even conjectured, at least with any plausibility, what the import was of either. Massmann, however, pronounced that the three of firwood, found in 1788 and deposited by Kovacs in the library at Clausenburg, were written in Latin and in the cursive character. He published in 1840 the Dissertation before referred to, in which he gave facsimiles of all the tablets, with a version and commentary of those on deal.

To justify his opinion that the character was a cursive form of the Latin, he traces, through known inscriptions, the gradual approximation of the lapidary and uncial to the cursive form. It is evident that a great change would take place, when the alphabet which had been used for inscriptions on brass or marble, came to be used for rapid writing on papyrus or wax. The oldest Latin MS. in existence is the poem before referred to (p. 174) on the battle of Actium, and from this to the earliest MS. of the classics which has come down to us, there is an interval of several centuries. The oldest is probably of the fifth century. These are in uncial letters, *i. e.*, capitals, being made no doubt by professional copyists. But we cannot doubt that a cursive character was in use, even in the times of the republic. Cicero surely did not carry on his voluminous correspondence in uncial characters. That the leaf of papyrus or the waxed tablet which the Romans used for rapid writing should have perished, is not surprising. In the change from an engraved to a written character some alteration would naturally take place, but this would be small compared with that involved in the formation of a *running hand*. A comparison of our printed characters with our ordinary writing will suggest what this change would be. Angles would give place to curves; letters would be joined, to save the loss of time involved in taking off the pen. A corresponding change is seen when we compare the Greek character in the papyri of the Ptolemaic times [1] with inscriptions of the same age, though the conversion into a running hand is not so complete in these, as in the waxed tablets. There is the same rounding and joining of the letters, but the characters are more coarse, being made with a reed pen, instead of a stylus. There was a strong antecedent probability that an inscription found in a Transylvanian mine would be in Latin. No other language spoken in that country probably has been reduced to writing till a recent period, and to this day the Wallachian language bears traces of the continuance of Roman dominion for a century and a half.

---

[1] Boeckh Erklärung einer Ægyptischen Papyrus in Griechischer cursivschrift. Berlin, 1821. Peyron Papyri Græci Regii Taurinensis Musei. Taurini 1826, 1827.

Massmann has pointed out another circumstance connected with the characters in which he supposes this inscription is written. The *reporters* (notarii) at Rome had a short-hand,[1] which from its use or invention by Tiro, the freedman of Cicero, is called Tironian notes.[2] They have been preserved in MSS.; they are evidently contractions from a written character, and several of the forms correspond with those of the Transylvanian tablets.

Their external form corresponds with the description of them in ancient writings. The fir tablets, which Massmann decyphered and interpreted, form a *triptych*, that is to say, they consist of three leaves, perforated at the side, and fastened together with thread, the remains of which are still visible. They thus formed what Ausonius, in the epigram quoted below, calls "bipatens pugillar," a handbook with two openings. The outer sides have no writing; the four inner pages are covered with wax, shrunk and blackened with age, and filled with writing, which in most places is still distinct. Altogether they very much resemble a modern memorandum book with double leaves.

The document inscribed on these tablets is evidently in duplicate. According to Massmann's interpretation, which will afterwards be given in detail, its purport is to declare, on the part of

---

[1] Martial, Epigr., 14, 208. "Currant verba licet, manus est velocior illis, Nondum lingua suam, dextra peregit opus." From Ausonius, Epig. 136, it appears that they used wax tablets. "Tu sensa nostri pectoris, Vix dicta jam coris tenes." According to Manilius (4, 197), in order to become a clever Notarius, "scriptor velox cui litera verbum est," it was necessary to be born under Virgo.

[2] See Gruter, Corp. Inscr., 4, Appendix, Notæ Tironis ac Senecæ. Kopp, Tachygraphia Veterum exposita et illustrata.

Artemidorus, who was the master of a college, or legalized association, consisting of fifty-four persons, formed for the purpose of contributing to funeral expences, that his colleague had not appeared at the college, that there was no money in hand, and that during a certain time, which appears to have been fixed by law, no one had paid a contribution. Consequently notice is given, that no application for burial money could be received. In the Appendix to a little work which I published on Roman Sepulcral Inscriptions,[1] I have given the rules of a Roman Burial Club: this document appears to record a break-up for want of funds. The notice was posted in a *statio*, one of those offices, in which questions of law were answered and legal documents prepared, and where the officers of the revenue transacted their business.[2]

The circumstances of the discovery of these tablets, the gradation traced by Massmann from the uncial to the cursive character, and the connected sense which they afford, as read and interpreted by him, might seem to remove all doubt of their genuine antiquity. Yet some eminent men have pronounced them a forgery. Letronne attacked them in the Journal des Savans of September 1841, immediately after the appearance of Massmann's book. A similar opinion was expressed by Silvestre, the author of the Palæographic Universelle, and supported by his colleague, Champollion Figeac,

---

[1] Roman Sepulcral Inscriptions, their Relation to Archæology, Language, and Religion. London, 1858, p. 65.

[2] See Facciolati, s. v. Statio. In mediæval Latinity it was used of an apothecary's or bookseller's shop; from the latter use comes our "Stationer." Du Cange, s. v.

who says, "Notwithstanding the care the modern inventor has taken to disguise his hand, by imitating with much skill the forms of certain letters, such as the *e* formed by two vertical lines and *a* and *d* as found in authentic documents, yet the indications of fraud are evident, the chief of which consists in the separation of the words, of which no example occurs, either in the longest Roman inscriptions, or in those monuments which are most analogous to them; in proof of which may be cited the Libellus of Velius Fidius, of the year 156 A. D., written in letters slightly rustic, unequal, conjoined, and somewhat approaching the cursive; a model, unfortunately for the wax tablets, so closely resembling them, as evidently to show the latter to be but disguised copies."

It is hardly logical to infer that a document is forged, because it closely resembles another unquestionably genuine, unless the marks of spuriousness are very palpable. The contrary inference is the fair one. There is no reason to suppose that the Libellus of Velius Fidius could have been known and copied in Transylvania in 1788, when the tablets in question first made their appearance. When it is said that in no Roman monuments is there any separation of the words, Champollion must mean, that where there is a separation it is marked by points, or an equivalent device, as almost any Roman inscription will show. When cursive writing began it was natural that these points, which really answered no purpose, should be dropped, and words be separated only by spaces. And if, with the view of imposing a spurious document on the world, a scholar had taken the pains to consult a genuine monument of the second century, how came he to overlook the want of separation between the words, and thus render his imitation imperfect?

It is natural also to ask, with what view was the forgery committed? Those who bestow labour on spurious antiquities have gain in view. And what labour must the author of this tablet have undergone! He must have carefully formed his alphabet by the study of a long series of Roman inscriptions, in which the changes of the letters appear. He must have initiated himself into Roman legal phraseology and antiquities, so as to give his Latin an archaic character and technical propriety. Last of all, he must have prepared a waxed tablet on which he scratched his forged document, and smoked it to the proper hue of antiquity. And what has he gained by his labour? In no instance of alleged discovery does any price appear to have been paid which could reward him. Those who employ their ingenuity in forgery copy some object, or class of objects, already known and valued— a Greek or Roman inscription, a unique coin, or gem; they produce a new work of a classic author, a poem of a mediæval monk, or a MS. play of Shakespear. But the assumed forger of the Transylvanian tablets could look neither for glory nor profit from the production of a work in a character and language about which, in 1788, no interest had been excited.

Letronne and Champollion were not the only palæographers who suspected the genuineness of the Massmann tablets. They were referred to as of authority, in the article "Tabulæ," of Dr. William Smith's Dictionary of Antiquities, and Sir Frederic Madden having seen this notice, in a letter addressed to the Editor of "Notes and Queries"[1] pronounced them to be forgeries, adding, that these very tablets *or similar ones,* were offered to him for purchase several years ago, but were rejected at once. They had been brought to his notice by Mr. Children, then Foreign Secretary to the Royal Society, to whom they appear to have been consigned from abroad. Sir Frederic's opinion of their spuriousness was founded very much, as I learn from a letter with which he favoured me, on the recent appearance of the wood in which the tablets were framed. This was in 1836—8, and therefore previous to the publication of Massmann's dissertation, by which the attention of archæologists was first called to this subject.

Subsequent discoveries have shewn that his suspicions were well founded, as regards the tablets offered to him. It has been mentioned that those which were found in 1788 were sold in 1834 to a trading antiquary, Samuel Nemes, and by him to Nicolas Jancovich, from whom they were purchased by the National Hungarian Museum at Pesth. These were on firwood, and they form the triptych which Massmann decyphered and explained. But the antiquary in question had sold at the same time to Jancovich, three other tablets, on beech wood, alleged to have been found in 1807 in a mine at Toroczkó. They are very different from the tablets

[1] See Notes and Queries of July 5, 1856.

on firwood. The character used in them is unknown. I am informed by Mr. Paget, that the vendor gave them out to be in Dacian or Hunno-Scythian characters. Whether he inscribed them at random, or imitated a character really found in the Szekler land, and supposed to be very ancient, is not known. No one professes to have read or interpreted them, and the probability is, that they are a pure invention. Massmann has given a facsimile of these, as well as of the fir tablets, but without professing to explain them. Nemes is said to have been a notorious fabricator of antiquities, and no doubt is entertained by the Hungarian archæologists, that he forged the beechen tablets. On one of them, a Greek hexameter verse, quoted in the second Alcibiades,[1] is inscribed three times, along with a fragment of prose by Aristobulus. Had these tablets been genuine, we might have supposed that this had been the *copy-book* of some school-boy, repeating a sentence as a writing exercise.[2] But the Greek character is quite modern, and I can only explain its appearance by supposing that Nemes, in his ignorance of palæography, had inscribed it with the design of increasing the interest of the tablet. On the fir tablets there is nothing of the kind.

Any doubt which may have existed in regard to the genuineness of the Latin tablets must be removed, by the recent discovery of others, photo-

---

[1] Found among the works of Plato, but generally admitted not to be his.

[2] St. Jerome, giving directions for the education of Læta, says, "Cum coeperit trementi manu *stilum in cera ducere*, alterius superposita manu teneri ligantur articuli." A Greek waxed tablet is in the British Museum with an iron stylus attached to it.

graphic copies of which I lay before the Society. A museum has lately been established in Clausenburg, to which contributions of antiquities have been made from various quarters, among them some waxed tablets, found in the mines near Veres Patak, in the mountainous district between Hungary and Transylvania. One of them, that which is best preserved, was discovered in 1855 by a Wallack miner, and was obtained for the museum without payment. The character is unmistakeably the same as that of Massmann's fir tablets. We have thus, according to the enumeration of Erdy, eight discoveries of waxed tablets, extending over a period of seventy years.[1] All have been made in similar circumstances, in the mines which we know to have been worked by the Romans. The idea of imposture therefore may be dismissed, and I have the authority of Sir Frederic Madden for saying, that he does not now impute forgery to any of the Latin tablets. We may advert to the contents of that which has been decyphered by Massmann, without fear of throwing away our time on a modern invention. A facsimile of one of the pages is given, copied from his work.

The general purport of the document has been already explained. At full length it runs thus:

Descriptum et recognitum factum ex libello qui propositus erat Alb. majori ad statione Resculi, in quo scriptum erat id quot (quod) i (infra) s (scriptum est).

Artemidorus Apolloni (filius) magister collegi Jovis Cerneni et Valerius Niconis (filius) et Offas Menofili quæstores Collegi ejusdem posito hoc libello publice testantur.

[1] De Tabulis ceratis in Transylvania repertis, p. 1—9.

Ex Collegio s (upra) s (cripto) ubi erant hom (ines) LIIII ex eis non plus remasisse [ad] Alb [urnum] quam quot h (omines) XI.

Julium Juli (filium) quoque commagistrum suum ex die magisteri sui non accessisse ad Alburnum neq in collegio seque eis qui præsentes fuerunt rationem reddedisse; et si quid eorum (h) abuerat reddidisset sive funeribus et cautionem suam in qua eis caverat recepisset modoque autem neque funeraticiis sufficerent neque loculum (h) aberet neque quisquam tam magno tempore diebus quibus legi continetur convenire voluerint aut conferre funeraticia sive munera.

Seque idcirco per hunc libellum publice testantur ut si quis defunctus fuerit, ne putet se collegium (h) abere aut ab eis aliquem petitionem funeris (h) abiturum.

Propositus Alb. majori v Idus Febr.

Imp L. AVR. VER. III et QVADRATO CS

Act [um] Alb. majori.

In English.

"Copied and revised, made from a notice which had been exhibited at the Greater Alburnum, in the office of Resculus, in which was written that which is written below.

"Artemidorus son of Apollonius, master of the College of Jupiter Cernenus, and Valerius son of Nicon, and Offas the son of Menofilus, quæstors of the said College, by this notice publicly declare.

"Of the College aforesaid, in which there were fifty-four men, of them no more remained at Alburnum than to the number of eleven.

"And that Julius, the son of Julius their colleague in the mastership, from the day of his [appointment to the (?)] mastership has not been at Alburnum nor in the College; and that they had rendered an account to those who were present; and if he had had anything of theirs he had given it back or [had expended it (?)] on funerals, and had received back the security which he had given to them; but that now neither were [the funds] sufficient for funeral expenses nor had he a coffin; and that in so long a time, within the days limited by law, no one had been willing to hold a meeting, or to contribute funeral expences or gifts.

"And therefore by this notice they publicly declare that if any [member] shall die he must not think that he belongs to the college or that he will have any right of demanding a funeral from them."

The general purport of this document is clear enough, and it is a strong presumption of its genuineness, that it relates to a subject so little known, as the burial clubs of the Romans. Alburnum is a place not ascertained in Transylvanian geography; but there can be no doubt of the correctness of the reading. The phrase with which it begins, "Descriptum et recognitum," is the formula with which an authenticated copy of a document deposited elsewhere is introduced, as in the "Honestæ missiones," the certificates of service and good conduct given to the Roman legionaries on their discharge.[1] The society or college was under the patronage of Jupiter Cernenus, as that of Lanuvium was established in honour of Diana and Antinous.[2] Jupiter had a variety of epithets,[3]

---

[1] Orelli No. 757, "Descriptum et recognitum ex tabula ænea quæ fixa est Romæ in Capitolio in ara gentis Juliæ." A decree of the people of Cære (Cervetri) corresponds still more closely with this proclamation of Artemidorus and his colleagues; Orelli 3797, "Descriptum et re cognitum factum ex commentario —in quo scriptum erat id quod infra scriptum est."

[2] Roman Sepulcral Inscriptions, u. s.

[3] See a collection of them in Orelli c. iv. "Jupiter Opt. Max. ejusque varia cognomina, etiam peregrina."

some derived from places in which he was worshipped, or in which the Romans found a divinity whom they identified with their own chief deity. As there was at Zerna, in Transylvania, a Roman colony, the name Cernenus probably refers to his worship and temple there.

The structure of the document is loose, Artemidorus sometimes speaking in the singular in his own name, sometimes in the plural in the joint names of himself and his colleagues. There is a ludicrous confusion of phrase in the concluding notice, that the deceased (si quis defunctus fuerit) must not fancy he had a claim on the club. *Seque* is followed by testantur, instead of testari. The suppression of the aspirate in *abere*, *abiturum*, and of the *n* in *remasisse*, shows a tendency to Italian forms, which the Latin language early manifested.[1] The genitive of the nouns in *ius* and *ium* is always in the contracted form, Apolloni, magisteri, &c. Statione is used for stationem, probably the result of a suppression of the letter *m* in pronunciation, which led to its elision in verse. The opposite page exhibits a lithographed facsimile of the commencement of the document, copied from Massmann's work. It is of the size of the original. In the wooden frame will be observed at *b* the remains of the twine, with which the three pieces of the triptych were fastened when it was closed. In the case of letters, the string was secured by a seal

---

[1] Roman Sepulcral Inscriptions, p. 23. It might perhaps be more correct to say, that these were dialectical forms of Latin, which, in the decline of the empire, obtained the ascendancy over the more polished idiom of the cultivated classes. See Max Müller, Lectures on the Science of Language, p. 56.

placed upon the knot, which was cut when they were opened.¹ The perforations at *l* and *k* were intended for the passage of wires to fasten the leaves together. These wires, of brass or iron, were still remaining in two of the tablets when they were discovered, much corroded by rust.² The page here given contains twelve lines, which read respectively as follows:—

1. Descriptum et recognitum factum ex libello qui propositus
2. Erat Alb majori ad statione Resculi in quo scriptum erat
3. Id quod i. s. est.
4. Artemidorus Apolloni magister collegi Jovis Cerneni et
5. Valerius Niconis et Offas Menofili questores collegi ejus
6. dem   Posito hoc libello publice testantur
7. Ex collegio s. s. ubi erant hom. L.IIII ex eis non plus
8. Remasisse ad Alb quam quot h. XI Julium Juli quoque
9. Commagistrum suum ex die magisteri sui non accessisse
10. Ad Alburnum neq in collegio   seque eis qui pro——
11. Sentes fuerunt rationem reddedisse et si quit
12. Eorum abuerat rededisset sive funeribus.

The ordinary forms of the Roman lapidary letters and the uncial letters of MSS. will readily be recognized in this cursive writing, allowance being made for the greater freedom with which characters are traced on wax, and the tendency, in a rapid use of the stylus or pen, to join letters to each other. The chief difference is that the letter *e* is made by two parallel strokes. This has its origin in the practice of expressing *e* by a double *ii*, which we find in numerous inscriptions, not only in the decline of the

---

¹ Cic. Catalin. 3, 5. "Tabellas proferri jussimus; Primum ostendimus Cethego signum; cognovit; nos linum incidimus; legimus." Plaut. Bacchides 4, 4, 63. "Effer cito stilum, ceram et tabellas et linum." 96, "Cedo tu ceram et linum actutum; age, obliga, obsigna cito." Pseudol. 1, 1, 40.

² Massmann, p. 25, note 2.

empire and in the catacombs, but even at Pompei, *e. g.*, ORNAMIINTIS; IIT for *et* BIINII MIIRIINTI for *bene merenti*,[1] one stroke is also made occasionally to do duty as part of two letters, in the manner of the ligatures which are so common in Roman inscriptions. With a little practice the character will be found easy to read.

The document is in duplicate. This repetition has contributed to the success of the decypherer, since the true nature of some characters obliterated in one page has been ascertained from the other.[2] The Lucius Aurelius Verus, whose name appears united with that of Quadratus in the date, was the unworthy brother of Marcus Antoninus; the year was that in which the Quadi and the Marcomcenni submitted themselves to Rome. The name Quadratus is of frequent occurrence in the Roman consular fasti. The colleague of Lucius Verus, was T. Numidius Quadratus.

To return to the photographs which gave occasion to this history of the previous discovery of waxed tablets. The originals of them were found in 1855 in the mine of St. Catherine, in the province of Vöröspatak, and three of them, which have been placed in the Clausenburg Museum, are represented in Mr. Paget's photographs, and in Erdy's Dissertation. The character in which they are written is precisely the same as that of the Massmann tablets, but they have not been so completely decyphered. They all appear to relate to

---

[1] Orelli, 4612, and in many other instances. The Greek η is sometimes substituted for the double *ii*.

[2] Massmann, p. 289.

contracts, and one of them, which bears date of the 13th day before the Kalends of November (October 20), in the second consulship of Rusticus and Aquilinus (A. D. 162), is a contract for a loan at interest. The oldest date is that of A. D. 139. On one of the pages the seals of seven witnesses still remain.[1] It is thus given by Mr. Finaly, the keeper of the Museum at Clausenburg, in a Report of the year 1861.[2] Some blanks have been filled up conjecturally, but of the general purport there can be no doubt.

Denarios sexsaginta qua die petierit probos recte dari fide rogavit Julius Alexander dari fide promisit Alexander Caricci et se eos denarios sexaginta qui supra scripti sunt mutuis numeratis accepisse et debere se dixit, et eorum usuras ex hac die in dies XXXII dari Julio Alexandro ea qua promisit fide rogavit Julius Alexander dari fide promisit Alexander Caricci.

Id fide sua esse jussit Titus Primitius dari sortem supra scriptam cum usuris promissis probe solutis.

Actum Alburno Majori XIII Kalendas Novembres.

Rustico II et Aquilino Consulibus.

Another relates to the purchase of a maiden for 205 denarii, warranted to be chaste and not a runaway. Another which is given by Mr. Finaly is an engagement on the part of a workman, who could not write, for labour in the gold mines, from the 20th of May to the 13th of November, with the stipulation that if he left work without leave he

---

[1] "And I saw in the right hand of him that sat on the throne a book, written within and on the back, sealed with seven seals." Rev. 5, 1.

[2] It is to be regretted that a patriotic reaction against the attempt of the Austrian government to force the German language upon the Hungarians, has led to the use of their own in publications of interest for European scholars generally. From this cause I am unable to give an account of the commentary with which Mr. Finaly has accompanied his copies of the inscriptions on the tablets.

should pay the contractor an *oclussis* (eight *asses*) a day; but that if he were obliged to stop working by an influx of water, the contractor was to pay *pro rata* for the time lost.

> Macrino et Celso Cos. xiii Kal. Junias Flavius Secundinus scripsi rogatus a Memmio Asclepi quia se literas scire negavit it quod dixit se locas . . . locavit operas suas opere aurario Aurelio adjutori . . . c. die . . Idus Novembres proxsimas . . ptaginta liberisque [laborisque?] . . . . . m per tempore accipere debebit s. as operas sanas va . ntes . . . debebit conductori s. s. quod si invito conductore . . cedere aut c. ssare voluer . . are debebit in dies singulos s. unum ere octus . . . . . . fluor impedierit pro rata conputare debeb . . conduct . . . tempore peracto mercedem solvendi moram fecerit ead . . . . tenebitur exceptis cessatis tribus.
> Actum Immenoso majori.

The consulship of M. Pompeius Macrinus and P. Juventius Celsus answers to A. D. 164.

These recent discoveries add something to our knowledge of Roman Antiquities, but their chief value is that they serve to dissipate any doubts which might remain of the genuineness of the Massmann tablets.

VIII.

NEW YEAR'S DAY IN ANCIENT ROME.

(Read Jan. 5th, 1864.)

ALTHOUGH we have passed the commencement of our civil year, the first day of our meeting here may be considered as the opening of our philosophical year, and the subject of this paper as not out of season.

Is there any such thing as a natural commencement of the year? Cosmically speaking, there is not. Our Earth moves with varying velocity, through different portions of her orbit, but she never halts even for a second, so that there is no starting point, no goal in her course. But the obliquity of her axis to the plane of her orbit, by producing the alternation of the seasons, exercises a direct influence on nature and man, and thus four points are fixed in her annual revolution, which have suggested the idea of the beginning or end of a period. These are the solstices and the equinoxes. Accordingly we find, that all these have, by different nations, been fixed upon for the beginning of a new year. The *maxima* and *minima* of light and heat, or the equality of their distribution, are so closely connected with man's comfort, that they afford an obvious division of the year. At first, probably, it was only in a vague way, as midwinter and midsummer, spring and autumn, that they were discriminated; but one of the earliest results of astronomical science must have been to fix these periods with approximate accuracy. Thales is said to have determined the exact solstitial and equinoctial points.[1]

The Egyptians, however, the oldest people of whose calendar we have any account, did not begin their year with any one of these four natural points. The first day of their first month, Thoth, was fixed by the heliacal rising of the brilliant star, Sirius or Sothis; *i. e.*, the time when it is sufficiently distant from the Sun to become visible in the morning before sunrise.[2] This distance is commonly fixed at 11°, but in the transparent atmosphere of Egypt 10° are said to be sufficient to make Sirius visible.[3] This answered in the year 139, A. D., to our 20th of July, and so it would do 1460 years before, at the commencement of the Sothiac period. And though it would not cor-

[1] Diogenes Laertius, 1, 23.   Handbuch der Chronol., 1, 127.
[2] Censorinus, c. 18.   Ideler,   [3] Ideler, 1, 129.

respond through the intermediate period, this day was reckoned as the commencement of the year. This time too coincides generally with the rise of the Nile, the beginning of the agricultural year to Egypt.

Upon the whole, the winter solstice, as the commencement of increasing light and heat,[1] and a season of comparative rest, seems most appropriate to the commencement of the year in temperate climates.

> "Hiems ignava colono,
> Frigoribus parto agricolæ plerumque fruuntur,
> Mutuaque inter se læti convivia curant."
> *Virg. Georg.*, 1, 299.

On the other hand, the Egyptian kept holiday and feasted in the dog days, his labours being suspended by the inundation.[2] Another consideration in fixing festival times, such as the commencement of the year, is indicated in Virgil's "parto fruuntur." A holiday implies a feast, and therefore it must take place when the materials of feasting are abundant. The Jewish Passover had no doubt an historical origin; but it could not have been kept except in the spring, when lambs and kids are plentiful. So the festivities of Halloween belong by their nature to the time when nuts and apples abound.

Whether astronomy was part of that "wisdom of the Egyptians in which Moses is said to have been learned" (Acts, 7, 22) we do not know; but there are no traces of such science in the Law, nor indeed till many centuries later, when the Jews became acquainted with the Babylonian

---

[1] Plutarch, Quæst. Rom., 18.   [2] Diod. Sic., 1, 36.

astronomy. Their own year began about the vernal equinox, like that of the Shemite Arabs and Syrians, its precise time being fixed by the date of their Exodus from Egypt, and the Feast of the Passover. Perhaps before this time it may have begun in autumn; at least the Feast of Ingathering, the close of the vintage, is called (Exod., 23, 16) the end (in the original *the outgoing*) of the year. The Persian year began at the vernal equinox.

Naturally the changes of the moon, which are so much more obvious than the motion of the Sun, were combined with the solstices and the equinoxes in fixing the beginning of the year. The Jewish months were lunar, and the year began with the new moon, of Abib, which was also the month of the Exodus. The Greeks, on the other hand, began their year with the first new moon after the summer solstice, and for this there was a good reason. The eleventh day of the moon was the time of the Olympic games, and as all Greece came together to them, it was not only desirable that they should be in midsummer, when the days were longest, but also when, from the moon's age, the nights were light, as the greater part of the visitors to Elis must have *camped out*.

The Roman year is said originally to have begun at the vernal equinox, and to have continued only ten months.[2] Ten months was the time during

---

[1] Exod. 13, 4.: Deut. 16, 1.
[2] "Tempora digereret quum conditor urbis, in orbe
Constituit menses quinque bis esse suo.
Quod satis est utero matris dum prodeat infans
Hoc anno statuit temporis esse satis.
Per totidem menses a funere conjugis uxor
Sustinet in vidua tristia signa domo."
Ovid Fasti, 1, 23.

which a widow was expected to wear her weeds, and not to marry again on pain of having to offer a cow in sacrifice. Till the year 153, B. C. (A. U. C. 601) the Consuls entered on their office at the Ides of March, and even when the day had been changed to the Kalends of January, the laurels before their doors were renewed on the former day. The Vestal fire was renewed on that day; the feast of the god Terminus was at the end of February, and the annual expiation of the sins of the year, and sacrifices in honour of the Manes (called Februa) took place then. These are plain indications of the close of the year, to which may be added that a day was intercalated at the end of February, in the bissextile year, and when the Romans had only a lunar year, an intercalary month. Certainly the names of the months Quintilis, Sextilis, September, &c., seem to imply a calendar in which March was the first. But at the time to which this paper refers, the Roman year had long been fixed to commence on the Kalends of January, and it is the customs of this day in Rome that I propose to illustrate. They are neither the same with our own nor altogether different. National customs bear an impress of national character, and hence their variety; they also take a special character from the climate, soil, traditions, literature, and religion of each country. And yet, with all these causes of variety, there is a remarkable amount of correspondence arising from the uniformity of human nature.

The two principal sources from which I propose to derive my illustrations are the Fasti of Ovid, and an antique terra cotta lamp, a wood-cut of which stands at the head of this paper.[1] Ovid's Fasti is a kind of poetical calendar, in which the fasts and festivals, the days sacred to the gods, the astronomical phenomena, the historical events belonging to each day in the first six months of the year, are described. It is uncertain whether the poet ever wrote the second half; at all events it has not reached us. The name Fasti, which we have borrowed, is derived from the distinction which the Romans made between the Dies fasti, the lucky days on which the Prætor was permitted *fari*, to speak, *i. e.*, pronounce his decrees; and the *nefasti* when he must be silent.[2] Hence the name became nearly equivalent to Calendar. It was extended to the chronological annals, which were marked by the succession of Consuls and other magistrates, and hence its application to lists of those who have filled high office. The lamp, though of clay, is of very elegant form; only its upper surface is here represented. As we proceed, we shall find so close a correspondence between its figures and inscription, and Ovid's account of the customs of New Year's Day, that we can hardly doubt that it has been a New Year's Gift in Ancient Rome.

Ovid represents himself as meditating, "sumptis tabellis," on the task which he had undertaken,

---

[1] The original is figured in Passeri's Lucernæ Fictiles, 1, 6, and in Millin's Galerie Mythologique, pl. 2, no. 5.

[2] "Ille Nefastus erit per quem tria verba silentur;
Fastus erit per quem lege licebit agi."
Fasti, 1, 47.

The *tria verba* were Do, Dico, Addico, the formulary words by which the Prætor prefaced his adjudications.

when the singularity of the form and attributes of Janus, who gave his name to the first month occurs to him, and he asks the god to explain his own form, to which nothing in Greek mythology corresponded; how he alone of all the celestials saw with his double head both what was before and what was behind him.

> "Quem tamen esse deum te dicam, Jane biformis?
> Nam tibi par nullum Græcia numen habet.
> Ede simul causam cur de cælestibus unus
> Sitque quod a tergo, sitque quod ante vides."

The god appears, holding a staff in the right hand and a key in the left; listens to him graciously, and assigns reasons for his own name and office. They are fanciful, as the reasons generally are, which the Greeks and Romans give for their own mythology; but in this case the nature of the symbols is obvious enough. Placed between two periods of time, one opening and one closing, the double face of Janus is a most appropriate emblem of the New Year. His epithets of *Clusius*, the shutter, and *Patulcius*, the opener, express the same thing. The most probable etymology of his name is that which Cicero gives,[1] *Eanus* from *eo* or *io*, *is*, *it* to go; janua being related to *io* as our gate is to *go*. He is a mere symbol, without personal qualities or history, to which circumstance, no doubt, he owes his blameless reputation; for St. Augustine remarks of him, that he was the only heathen god,

---

[1] Ab *eundo* nomen est ductum, ex quo transitiones perviæ *Jani* foresque in limine ædium *januæ* nominantur. Cic. N. D., 2, 27. Macrobius derives it from Dianus, on the authority of Nigidius, a learned antiquary, who identified him with Apollo, and gave him Diana as the Moon for a sister. Saturn, 1, c. 9.

of whom no scandal was related.¹ The meaning of his form being so obvious, we need not, with Sir Wm. Jones, seek his origin in the Indian god Ganesa, or with the learned Vossius, suppose that he represents Noah, looking with one head backward on the antediluvian world, and forward with the other on the postdiluvian, or that he was the same with Javan, whose descendants peopled Europe.² He was one of the old Italian gods, the Dii Indigetes,³ on whom neither poetry nor art had exercised their plastic powers. Ovid, it is true, puts a staff into his right hand, and a key into his left,—one to support his aged steps—for Time is always made an old man,—the other, to denote his office of opening and closing. But these are embellishments. The true Janus is a double-headed bust, or a square pillar surmounted with two heads, and it is only on imperial coins that we find him represented with a perfect human figure.⁴ Pliny (34, 16) speaks of figures of Janus, with the fingers disposed in such a way as to express the number 355, the days in a lunar year (Macrobius says, Sat., 1, 9, 365); and Venerable Bede has written a treatise on this digital arithmetic (Op. 1, 164); but no such figure of Janus has come down to us.

Ovid then proceeds to ask Janus, why the year has been made to begin in the depth of winter, and not in the more genial season of spring?

> "Dic age frigoribus quare novus incipit annus
> Qui melius per ver incipiendus erat?"

---

[1] De Jano quidem non mihi facile occurrit quidquam, quod ad probrum pertineat. De Civ. Dei, 7, 4.

[2] G. J. Vossius, de Idol., 1, 18.
[3] Herodian, 1, 49.
[4] Medal of Antoninus Pius. Cohen, 874. Rasche, 2, 2, p. 511.

Janus answers that *bruma*, a contraction of *brevima* (shortest day), is the last day of the old and first of the new sun, and that Phœbus and the year begin together. "Bruma novi prima est veterisque novissima solis Principium capiunt Phœbus et annus idem." This is not strictly true of the first of January, which is ten days later than the winter solstice, but it is near enough for the Poet's purpose. The shortening of the shadow of the gnomon, by which the Romans were guided, was scarcely perceptible for eight or ten days after the solstice.[1] Our Gothic ancestors not only began their years in winter, but reckoned them by winters. In the version of Ulfilas (Luke 2, 42), "And when he was twelve years old" is, "Jah bi thê warth twalib wintrus." So the Lindisfarn Gospel, "wintra tuoelf."

The poet then proceeds to the customs of the day and their reasons. "Why are the law courts open though it is a holiday?" "Because, for the sake of a good omen, every one should, on the first day of the year, just handle his tools," a process which in Latin was called *delibare*.

> "Post ea mirabar cur non sine litibus esset
>   Prima dies. Causam percipe, Janus ait.
> Tempora commisi nascentia rebus agendis,
>   Totus ab auspicio ne foret annus iners.
> Quisque suas artes ob idem delibat agendo
>   Nec plus quam solitum testificatur opus."

This rule seems to have been universal. The farmer on this day did a slight stroke of work in

---

[1] Lydus de Mensibus, 2, 12.

every department of his farm; the literary man, as we learn from Seneca,[1] read a little, wrote a little, spoke a little; the prætor pronounced judgment in some formal matter, but did not exercise his contentious jurisdiction, lest the wrangling of the bar should lead to the utterance of ill-omened words.

> "Prospera lux oritur: linguis animisque favete:
> Nunc dicenda bono sunt bona verba die.
> Lite vacent aures, insanaque protinus absint
> Jurgia; differ opus livida lingua tuum."

This was so carefully avoided, that on all critical occasions silence was enjoined to prevent its possibility, and *favere lingua* was equivalent to *holding your peace*. Ill-omened actions were avoided, as well as ill-omened words; no executions took place, and even Christians were not put to death on the Kalends of January as St. Jerome notices. It was an evil omen, that on the morning of New Year's Day, the Consul Norbanus, who was learning to play on the trumpet, blew a blast of war. The statue of Janus fell down, and in that year Germanicus died (Dion., 59, c. 17). The senate observed the same rule. The new Consuls took possession of their curule chair, or as Ovid expresses it, "the ivory felt a new weight;" but no important business was commonly entered upon. It was a mark of Cicero's eagerness to denounce the Agrarian Law, proposed by the tribune Rullus, that he delivered an harangue against it, on the Kalends of January, the very day of his entrance upon office.

[1] Ep. 83.

All on this day in Rome wore the appearance of festivity. White was the festive colour, and the citizen who could not afford a new toga, at least whitened his old one, to attend the sacrifices in the Capitol. Lydus says, the Consul rode a white horse and offered him to Jupiter.[1] This probably belongs to later times and the worship of the Sun. The Consuls robed in new garments, bordered with purple, went thither, preceded by lictors carrying the new fasces wreathed with laurel.

"Vestibus intactis Tarpeias itur in arces
    Et populus festo concolor ipse suo est.
Jamque novi præeunt fasces, nova purpura fulget
    Et nova conspicuum pondera sentit ebur."

When I was in Rome on New Year's Day, and saw the long procession of Cardinals, clothed in scarlet from head to foot, with scarlet liveries and scarlet harness, going to pay their homage at the Vatican, I could not but recollect the "nova purpura fulget" of Ovid, and suspect that they had inherited the senatorial purple. After sacrificing in the Capitol, the chief magistrates had an audience of the Emperor, and a kiss was interchanged. The troops also mustered with their ensigns, and both in Rome and the provinces they renewed the military oath, or *sacramentum*.[2] It was a mad freak of Commodus, which cost him his life, instead of appearing in imperial purple on this day, to head a band of gladiators in their professional costume.[3]

The poet next inquires, "why do we reciprocate

---

[1] De Mens, 4, c. 3.
[2] Lydus, 4. c. 4.
[3] Herodian, 1, 49. Lucian, Pseudologista, c. 8. speaks of the third day from the Kalends, as that on which good wishes were interchanged. Plutarch, Vit. Ciceronis, c. 2.

good wishes and cheerful words on this day?" He does not tell us what the form was, but the monuments supply them. "ANNUS NOVUS SIT TIBI FAUSTUS FELIX," or without the verb "ANNUM NOVUM FAUSTUM FELICEM TIBI." "May the new year be auspicious and happy to thee!" Such is the form in which it appears on two tesseræ, figured by Caylus, and which no doubt were *sent* by those who had not the opportunity of uttering their good wishes in person.[1] On this lamp it is Anno novo, so that *faustum* and *felix* must be taken as substantives. This question having been answered by saying "omina principiis inesse solent," Ovid asks the meaning of the various gifts which friends present to each other on New Year's Day. "What means the palm, and the wrinkled Carian fig, and the pure honey given in the white jar?" Instead of a jar of honey, as seen on this lamp, a cake made with honey was sometimes given.[2] The gifts presented on this day passed by the general name of *strenæ*, a word of doubtful etymology, but which seems originally to have denoted the branch of a sacred evergreen shrub, which constituted the simple new year's gift. It survives, in the latter sense, in the Italian *strenna* and the French *étrennes*. Janus answers, "the object of giving sweet things is that a flavour of sweetness may attend the year through its whole course." We find from Martial, that dates, as well as figs, were given as *strenæ*, along with the

[1] Caylus, Recueil d'Antiquités 4, 286. Passeri 2, pl. 4, 5. Fabretti, Inscr. Domesticæ, c. 7, no. 5.

[2] Lydus, u. s. The lump of figs is seen beside the head of Victory.

branch of the palm, the fruit being covered with gold leaf.[1]

> "At cur læta tuis dicuntur verba Kalendis
>   Et damus alternas accipimusque preces?
> Tum deus incumbens baculo, quem dextra gerebat
>   Omina principiis, inquit, inesse solent.
> Ad primam vocem timidas advertitis aures
>   Et primum visam consulit augur avem.
> Templa patent auresque deûm, nec lingua caducas
>   Concipit ulla preces, dictaque pondus habent.
> Desierat Janus; nec longa silentia feci,
>   Sed tetigi verbis ultima verba meis.
> Quid vult palma sibi, rugosaque carica dixi,
>   Et data sub niveo candida mella cado?
> Omen, ait, causa est, ut res sapor ille sequatur
>   Et peragat cœptum dulcis ut annus iter."

The poet is satisfied with the reason assigned for giving sweets, but goes on to ask, "why is a small piece of money" (*stips*, whence *stipendium*) "also given?" Janus replies by laughing at Ovid's ignorance of the character of his own times, in which money was held to be the sweetest of all sweet things; and he goes on satirically to contrast the simplicity of primitive times (for of course his memory extended to all past ages), when senators fed their own sheep, and slept on straw, with the luxury and venality of the moderns.

> "Dulcia cur dentur video, stipis adjice causam,
>   Pars mihi de festo ne labet ulla tuo.
> Risit, et O! quam te fallunt tua sæcula dixit
>   Qui stipe mel sumpta dulcius esse putes.
> Vix ego Saturno quemquam regnante videbam
>   Cujus non animo dulcia lucra forent.

[1] Epigr. 13, 27, Aurea porrigitur Jani caryota Kalendis, Sed tamen hoc munus pauperis esse solet, a cheap but showy present, Comp. 8, 33.

> Tempore crevit amor, qui nunc est summus habendi ;
> Vix ultra, quo jam progrediatur habet."

In another lamp, figured by Passeri (1, 5), the head of Janus is surrounded by coins of all kinds. The *stips* was usually a piece of copper money, and especially one of those of the earliest brass coinage, which exhibited the head of Janus on one side, and the prow of a vessel on the other.[1] The obverse side is seen on the lamp. The Emperors did not disdain these humble offerings. If Augustus was absent on New Year's Day, the *stips* was deposited in the Capitol, and from the sums received he dedicated statues to the gods.[2] Tiberius stood to receive it in person, and returned it fourfold, but confined it strictly to the first of January.[3] Caligula seems to have revived the practice for the purpose of getting money, though, as Suetonius says, he was literally rolling in gold.[4] Our own sovereigns in the Middle Ages received and sometimes exacted New Year's gifts from the courtiers and the citizens. Matthew Paris (s. a. 1249) mentions such a demand by Henry III. on the citizens of London.

Some other objects appear upon the lamp, to which Ovid does not allude. Below the coin are two fruits, perhaps pomegranates, and on the right hand of the Victory a pine-cone. This would not

---

[1] The prow is said to refer to Saturn, who, as representing Time, was easily confounded with Janus, and supposed to typify his arrival by sea in Latium. The Romans seem, however, to have borrowed their earliest copper money from the Etruscans, to whom as a maritime people, the emblem of the prow would be appropriate. See Inghirami, Monumenti Etruschi, vol. 3, pl. 1—5.

[2] Suetonius, Octavianus, c. 57.

[3] Suet. Tib., c. 43.

[4] Suet. Calig., c. 42. "Sæpe super immensos aureorum acervos et nudis pedibus spatiatus et toto corpore aliquandiu volutatus est."

with us be reckoned among fruits; but the cone of the stone-pine is sold as such in Italy. It is covered indeed with an impenetrable coat of mail, but the fire opens it, and there are kernels within of a sweet taste, like that of a nut. A curious story is related by Macrobius, respecting this *nux pinea*. Vatinius (the same no doubt against whom Cicero delivered a tremendous invective) had been pelted with stones, during an exhibition of gladiators, and had persuaded the ædiles to make a regulation, that only *poma*, by which soft fruits were meant, should be used as missiles during the performances in the arena. For the ancient Romans seem to have used the same licence of pelting during the games, that the moderns do at the Carnival. Cascellius, a celebrated lawyer, was consulted, as to whether the cone of the pine was a *pomum* or not, and replied: "If you mean to pelt Vatinius with it, I hold it to be a *pomum*."[1]

Hitherto we have been contemplating the poetical and religious side of New Year's Day in ancient Rome. No doubt, if we could follow the population of the great metropolis through the day, we might find things less edifying. Joannes Lydus, a late writer says, that the Pontiffs, on the authority of the Sibylline books, enjoined on the people, the first thing in the morning of the Kalends of January, to take a drink of pure wine, for the avoidance of gout;[2] but, doubtless, it was not the only cup that was taken during the day. Those who are fond of tracing customs from one country

---

[1] Macrobius, Saturn., 2, c. 6.   [2] Lydus, De Mensibus, 4, c. 8.

to another, may find a parallel to this in the practice which prevailed, and may still prevail, in Scotland, of going into your friend's house, on the morning of New Year's Day, with a bottle of whisky in your hand, and giving a glass to the inmates before they left their bed. Intoxication, however, has never been the national vice of the Italians, and the allegation of a sanitary reason for taking a cup of pure wine, the first thing in the morning, shows that such an indulgence was not common. The same authority (Lydus, 4, c. 57) prescribed, that on the Kalends of June, a drink of cold water should be taken the first thing in the morning, and that, too, for the very same reason, the avoidance of gout. Whatever may have been the case in the better times of Rome, the festival of the *strenæ* seems to have become an occasion of licence. The fathers of the Church are very bitter against it; for it was connected with idolatrous worship, besides being an occasion of licence and misrule.[1] "You are about (says St. Augustine) to engage in the celebration of the strenæ after the Pagan manner; to game and be intoxicated. How can you believe, or hope, or love? They give strenæ; do you give alms. They are singing loose songs; do you occupy yourselves with the words of Scripture. They run to the theatre; do you go to Church. They are intoxicated; do you fast." Pope Zacharias, in the eighth century, pronounced an anathema on those who lighted lamps,

---

[1] See Bingham, Antiquities of the Christian Church, 7, 257. Montacutius (Bp. Montague). Orig., 1, 128. Hospinian, De Origine Festorum. Brand, Popular Antiquities, ch. 16.

and prepared feasts on this day, and went about singing and dancing in the streets, a practice of which our waits and carols no doubt preserve a trace. The Feast of the Circumcision was instituted to change the character of the day. Our mummers owe their origin, also, to the disguising, and especially interchange of the garments of the sexes at this season, which was severely condemned by the Synod held *in Trullo*. The *strenæ* became an occasion of extravagance. St. Jerome complains (Comm. Ep. ad Ephes.) that bishops and priests spent on New Year's gifts, the offerings or fines of maidens and widows. But as New Year's Day, in Protestant countries, is not a day of suspension of business, the gifts and the feasting have been anticipated by Christmas Day, and little more than good wishes have been left to the Kalends of January. In France, on the contrary, it is celebrated by a universal interchange of gifts, and the *Jour des étrennes*, is one of the liveliest of the year.

There was one class of persons at Rome, to whom the Kalends of January was anything but a festival. The first day of the month was that on which the creditor could demand his debt with the pawnbroking interest of one per cent. for the month, *i. e.*, 12 per cent. per annum, and the Kalends of January would be doubly dreaded as the first of the year as well as the month. The *calendarium* was the book in which the usurer inscribed a list of the names of his debtors, and the amount of their debts. "He who has a great *calendarium*" says Seneca, "is a rich man."[1] His own must have

[1] De Benef., 7, 87, 6.

been of extraordinary size; for though a Stoic in theory, and therefore a despiser of riches, he was at Rome, what the Fuggers of Augsburg were in the sixteenth century, what the Rothschilds are in the nineteenth,—the great loan-monger of his time. He was reputed to have amassed, in four years, £2,500,000 sterling.[1] The rebellion of the Britons under Boadicea was brought about by his harshly and suddenly calling up the loans which he had lent them, to the amount of £330,000.[2]

The Roman insolvent debtor was not in so lamentable a condition in the imperial times as under the law of the Twelve Tables, by which his creditors might literally take his body in execution, and make a dividend of it among them if they chose. But the consequences of insolvency were sufficiently serious, to make the approach of the Kalends a gloomy prospect; for the *nexus* against whom his creditor had obtained judgment, became in all but name his slave. The Greeks had no Kalends, but to them the day of dread was the new moon, on which debts were to be discharged. Aristophanes, in The Clouds (739), represents a man, who being deeply in debt, is in sore perplexity at the approach of the new moon. He has heard that Thessalian hags have power by certain incantations to draw the moon down from the heavens (carmina vel cœlo possunt deducere lunam), and he is in hopes of finding one with a spell sufficiently

---

[1] " Qua sapientia, quibus philosophorum præceptis, intra quadriennium ter millies sestertium paravisset? Romæ testamenta et orbos, velut indagine ejus capi. Italiam et provincias immenso fœnore hauriri." Tac., Ann., 13, 42.

[2] Dion. Cass., lib. 62, c. 2.

powerful to bring her into his safe keeping, and so enable him to set his creditors at defiance.

If a sculptor were to attempt to give appropriate expression to the stony faces of Janus, the head which looks to the future should bear the marks of anxious curiosity; for such is the feeling with which man enters on a new period of his life. And as no philosophy can relieve him from this uncertainty, he has had recourse to superstition, trying to find a shadow of coming events in the fortuitous circumstances of the opening year, and, above all, in the phænomena of the heavens. Trajan chose the first of January for the consecration of a Temple to Fortune, doubtless, in order to make the goddess propitious for the coming year. It was the duty of the Consuls to report to the Emperors on this day, what the auguries declared respecting its character, which depended very much on the day of the week on which New Year's Day fell. They would have given gloomy anticipations of 1864; for if the year begins on a Friday, they held that you may look for a good harvest, but must be prepared for political tumults, burdensome wars, and murders of magistrates.[1]

I have not found traces in the classic authors of any evil augury attaching to a bissextile year (so called because the 24th of February, sixth before the Kalends of March, in Roman reckoning, was counted twice), but the bissextile day itself was reckoned so unlucky, that Valentinian, having been elected Emperor, would not shew himself in public till after the 24th of February was past. Ammianus Marcellinus, who mentions this, says it was

[1] Lydus, 4, 10.

because he knew that the day had been several times unlucky for Rome, but mentions no particulars. St. Augustine, who was nearly contemporary with Valentinian, complains of the superstitious dread attached to the bissextile year, which must have been prevalent among the Christians of his day, since he rebukes them by the words of St. Paul to the Galatians (4. 10), "Ye observe days, and months, and times, and years." "What folly!" he exclaims, to say, "I will not plant a vineyard this year, because it is bissextile."[1] Dithmar, the Bishop of Merseburg, in the tenth century, alludes to the opinion, and seems himself to have been under its influence.[2] Ordericus Vitalis,[3] in a passage kindly pointed out to me by Mr. Raine, speaking of the year 1136, and King Stephen, says, "Hic tumultuosus annus *vere bissextus* fuit et tunc ultimus in ordine concurrentium bissextus cucurrit, sicut vulgo dicitur, bissextus super regem et populum ejus in Normannia et Anglia cecidit." The superstition must have been very prevalent in the fifteenth century, since Battista Spagnuola, who, under the assumed name of Mantuanus, wrote numerous Latin poems, and one in particular, called Fasti, notices and ridicules it, and maintains that on the contrary, as Time is a good thing, the longer the year the better.

"Felicior isto
Judice me credi debet quia longior annus.
Scilicet in silvis arbor magis ardua fertur
Dignior; in caulis taurus præstantior alta
Cui cervice magis caput a tellure levatum est."

[1] Epist., 119, Ad Januarium, c. 7.
[2] Hospinian, De Origine Festorum, p. 31.
[3] Duchesne, Hist. Normann. Scriptores, 905. Compare Lingard, 2, p. 230—33.

It is not easy to ascertain the origin of this ancient superstition. Perhaps it sprang from the feeling, that intercalation was an act of impiety—an interference of man with the laws of the universe. The alteration of the style in England in 1753, we know, was regarded in that light by the common people. Whether a leap-year is still held by them to threaten calamity, except to bachelors, I do not know. Superstitions are tenacious of life and long resist the influence of education. To my present audience, however, I may safely address the old Roman salutation and wish, "ANNUS NOVUS SIT VOBIS FAUSTUS FELIX," though 1864 began on a Friday, and though February will have twenty-nine days. Philosophy has shown us, that human destinies are not controlled by the position and aspects of the heavenly bodies, and Religion has provided a remedy for undue anxiety respecting the future, by teaching us to look forward to it with trust and resignation.

www.ingramcontent.com/pod-product-compliance
Lightning Source LLC
Chambersburg PA
CBHW031733230426
43669CB00007B/338